PUBLISHING IN THE DIGITAL AGE

The world of publishing is evolving at an ever-increasing speed, with developments in digital workstreams and products, customer expectation, enriched content curation, and user-generated content becoming commonplace. In *Publishing in the Digital Age: How Business Can Thrive in a Rapidly Changing Environment*, Ross discusses the most significant and recent developments in educational and trade publishing, educational technology, and marketing that has enabled a new generation of content creators to reach more consumers. It is the only book that addresses disruption in the industry head on.

Building on the insights from his last book, *Dealing with Disruption: Lessons from the Publishing Industry*, Ross takes a fresh look at the publishing environment and provides the reader with a clear view of how publishing has evolved and how it has benefitted consumers regardless of their preferred medium for accessing knowledge. Through an examination of what has worked and what has not, and with Ross's unique perspective of more than 35 years of publishing success, *Publishing in the Digital Age* presents an indispensable overview of the publishing industry, how it has evolved during the first quarter of the 21st century, and how publishers, content providers, and consumers can benefit from the many options that are available today. With insights from industry leaders, Ross discusses new opportunities on the Web, streaming services, and audio formats. He reviews new publishing platforms and provides a practical guide for content developers to address the knowledge needs of their constituents by giving readers real-life, actionable examples of how best to publish their content consistent with users' purchasing preferences.

The book will be of interest to specialists in education: K-12 and higher education, the non-fiction trade, corporate education trainers, and specialist sectors such as scholarly, technical, and medical publishing. It includes clear applications for any business that is undergoing transformation or is forced to make a radical pivot because of sudden environmental changes or market conditions.

Michael N. Ross is the President/Founder of Ross & Associates LLC, an educational publishing and technology consultancy. Before establishing Ross & Associates in 2017, Michael was the SVP and Education GM at Encyclopaedia Britannica, Inc., where he led the sales and marketing activities in North America and EMEA and ran the product development and technology teams. Prior to joining Britannica in 2002, he was the EVP and Publisher of World Book, Inc. and previously held executive positions at other global publishing companies. He began his career as an editor for Time-Life Books, including three years in Tokyo.

PUBLISHING IN THE DIGITAL AGE

How Business Can Thrive in a Rapidly Changing Environment

Michael N. Ross

LONDON AND NEW YORK

First published 2022
by Routledge
2 Park Square, Milton Park, Abingdon, Oxon OX14 4RN

and by Routledge
605 Third Avenue, New York, NY 10158

Routledge is an imprint of the Taylor & Francis Group, an informa business

© 2022 Michael N. Ross

The right of Michael N. Ross to be identified as author of this work has been asserted by him in accordance with sections 77 and 78 of the Copyright, Designs and Patents Act 1988.

All rights reserved. No part of this book may be reprinted or reproduced or utilised in any form or by any electronic, mechanical, or other means, now known or hereafter invented, including photocopying and recording, or in any information storage or retrieval system, without permission in writing from the publishers.

Trademark notice: Product or corporate names may be trademarks or registered trademarks, and are used only for identification and explanation without intent to infringe.

British Library Cataloguing-in-Publication Data
A catalogue record for this book is available from the British Library

Library of Congress Cataloging-in-Publication Data
A catalog record has been requested for this book

ISBN: 978-0-367-75483-9 (hbk)
ISBN: 978-0-367-75484-6 (pbk)
ISBN: 978-1-003-16263-6 (ebk)

DOI: 10.4324/9781003162636

Typeset in Joanna
by codeMantra

To

Thomas John Murphy (1931–2012)
publisher, friend, mentor, humanist, volunteer

Kathleen Schultz
wife, mother, editor, educator, sainthood candidate—for putting up with me

CONTENTS

List of figures   ix
List of tables   x
Also by Michael N. Ross   xi
Preface   xii

Introduction: our analog past   1
Numbers and words, people and places   2
Knowledge most worth owning   9
Paper thin and bound to end   12

1   **The 21st-century publisher: bridging millennial formats**   27
Print is dead, long live print   27
Solving the print dilemma digitally   35

2   **Print and digital hybrids: first inklings**   40
Conversion pains   45
Transition, transition!   49

3   **Data, metadata, and humans**   53
Digital first, but not last   54
Behind the paywall   57

4	**EdTech: closing the digital divide**	**64**
	Byte-sized learning	66
	Digital finds a platform	73
	EdTech meets a real "bug"	76
	Training squeals	80
5	**Keeping the customer satisfied**	**86**
	Churn low, retain high	87
	Great expectations	93
	Over here, over there	97
6	**First, identify the problem**	**103**
	Youth communication: amplifying powerful young voices	108
	Open sesame	116
7	**The media and the message**	**121**
	Making it happen	128
	Me, myself, and I	130
8	**"Palaces for the people" and their treasures**	**137**
	Palace squabbles	140
	Keys to the kingdom	144
	Trusted sources	147
9	**"Information (almost) wants to be free"**	**154**
	What price is right?	155
	Epilogue: back to the future	**161**
	The scent of film	162
	Digital now!	166
	From tactile to digital	170
	Index	179

FIGURES

6.1	Directory Layout 1	106
6.2	Final Directory Layout	107
8.1	Media Interface	149
8.2	Database Interface	150
8.3	Online Courses Interface	150
E.1	UV&S Salt Mine	163
E.2	Entrance to the Britannica Vault at UV&S	164
E.3	Charles Benton in the Britannica Vault at UV&S	165

TABLES

3.1	Search Term: Space	60
4.1	K-12 Teacher Comments	67
4.2	LMS Features and Benefits	75
5.1	Publishing and EdTech Lexicon	95
9.1	Sample Pricing Models	158

ALSO BY MICHAEL N. ROSS

Publishing without Borders: Strategies for Successful International Publishing
Publishing without Boundaries: How to Think, Work, and Win in the Global Marketplace
Dealing with Disruption: Lessons from the Publishing Industry

PREFACE

In 2007, I wrote a book entitled *Publishing without Boundaries: How to Think, Work, and Win in the Global Marketplace*, which had two main objectives: To provide publishers with editorial strategies for creating culturally appropriate products for non-traditional markets, and to outline ways to leverage emerging digital technologies to generate additional revenue streams. The book provides a roadmap for how publishers can break through the outmoded constraints of their usual geographic and format "boundaries" to maximize the initial investments they make in their intellectual properties and encourages publishers "to look beyond ink on paper and to take advantage of the digital options that were available at the time. Opportunities in new markets, foreign and domestic, and in new formats were not being fully exploited." Even though much of what I discussed in that book remains relevant, the strategies I recommended that publishers employ for developing their business plans are insufficient for today's rapidly evolving, technology-driven environment.

Over the past 15 years, publishers have had a variety of technology options available to help improve their business fundamentals and to meet market requirements. Although publishers have recognized that to remain relevant, they would need to adopt digital technologies more aggressively than in the past, it was not always clear which solutions would have staying power and were less likely to be obsolesced in the near term. Publishers as well as their customers have become wary of committing to new formats, as early adopters of previous technologies often discovered that they had made the wrong choice. Even the savviest decisionmakers could be lured into making a bet on a losing horse.

Unknowingly choosing a technology at the end of its lifecycle can be costly in terms of lost time and wasted resources. Unfortunately, we have seen this scenario occur frequently in the education sector, where publishers and their customers have burned through a series of analog and digital formats, wasting hardware and software purchases, in a short time span. All too often, as soon as a publisher had completed the implementation of a tech solution, and before the investment could be amortized on the balance sheet, it was time to move on to another one.

Over the course of a 40-year career in publishing, I have developed and brought to market products in nearly every popular format, most of which now belong to the annals of publishing history. Educational films, produced on celluloid and played on 16-mm film projectors, as well as 35-mm filmstrips, which utilized their own dedicated hardware—widely distributed in schools and libraries in the 1960s through the first-half of the 1980s and then in VHS and DVD formats in the 1990s—accounted for a miniboom in publishing. Laserdiscs (an analog technology despite its digital-sounding name) emerged as a competing format for a short time in the 1980s, only to be superseded by VHS and Betamax tapes, and then CD-ROMs and DVDs. When the personal computer arrived, schools and libraries established separate spaces for computer labs, and then transitioned to building-wide local area networks (LANS), which in turn were largely supplanted by interactive whiteboards and tablets in classrooms.

Print has survived through the decades and remains a standard in the consumer and education markets today, along with Internet devices that provide users access to multimedia content—including streaming video—from the "cloud" (a collection of servers, often in multiple locations). On a large scale, the education sector has adopted the use of Web-based learning management systems (LMS), or learning content management systems (LCMS) that store, organize, and deliver proprietary school-district content, shared content with other connected servers, and downloadable content from the Web.

Regardless of their target market, publishers have become entirely dependent on access to accurate and up-to-date information and knowledge on the Web, either through free Web services or proprietary sites behind paywalls. We may not be able to imagine what if anything will replace the Internet, but we can safely assume that the devices and software that provide us with almost instant access to cloud content will continue to feature faster processing speeds, more memory, better screen resolution, and advanced functionality to respond to an increasingly competitive environment and consumer preferences.

Rapidly changing technologies have presented a challenge to publishers in meeting both their customers' needs and business objectives. No one wants to get caught with their trends down, but a publisher should not have to go bankrupt while keeping up with advances in technology. Other businesses have faced similar challenges in adopting technology solutions. Threats to traditional businesses from unconventional innovators have meant that business leaders have been forced to adjust their tactics quickly or choose between undesirable options—including selling off assets or shutting down altogether.

Meanwhile, agile startups bursting on the scene with better mousetraps or more efficient ways to meet the needs of consumers have been poised to take advantage of opportunities that traditional businesses were either too slow to embrace or simply ignored. If traditional businesses, including most publishers, were to thrive in this fast-moving environment, they would need to alter their business practices and phase out aging or antiquated methodologies. Consumers are fickle, and loyalty has a price. Businesses must be prepared to abandon outdated practices that do not adequately respond to shifting market expectations.

In 2016, I wrote *Dealing with Disruption: Lessons from the Publishing Industry* "to help publishers in particular—and businesses in general—take advantage of new opportunities that have resulted from innovation in product development, production, and manufacturing, as well as the wider use of the Internet." I identify publishing strategies that enable companies to improve their business models by eliminating inefficient processes, adopting more reliable technology solutions, and establishing alliances with alternative distribution partners. In an industry that was undergoing a paradigm shift from predominantly print-based products to digital solutions, successful publishers formed alliances with "disruptive vendors in the supply chain that have gone from being upstarts to entrenched businesses," and, as we have seen in some cases over the last five years or so, dominant, megabillion-dollar (even trillion-dollar) global enterprises.

Dealing with Disruption outlines creative marketing models and original product categories that emerge when traditional business models get disrupted—sometimes replaced—by cutting-edge technologies. One classic example is the demise of the video rental business, which was displaced by streaming services. Blockbuster, the largest brand in video rental, opened its first storefront in 1985, began to lose relevancy when Netflix went public in 2002, filed for bankruptcy in 2010, and finally shuttered completely in 2014—a relatively short timeline from sunrise to sunset given Blockbuster's hegemony in the video market. However, by not recognizing weaknesses in existing business models and the benefits (e.g., convenience, price, choice) of alternative models, many companies experienced a similar decline. Ernest Hemingway captures this type of downturn in *The Sun Also Rises* when Mike Campbell replies to Bill Gorton's question to him on how he went bankrupt: "Two ways, gradually and then suddenly."

Disruptive technology does not always cause total collapse like the Blockbuster/Netflix example, or at least not as quickly. In the late 1990s, Amazon upended the brick-and-mortar bookstore business with a stunningly efficient direct-to-consumer online delivery service, but it did not eliminate bookstores altogether, nor did it remain the only online bookseller. Although the physical bookstore business as epitomized by national chains is no longer what it used to be—and at one point was regarded like the dinosaur, soon to become extinct— today, independent booksellers, selling new and used books, are experiencing something of a renaissance, and in many small towns and suburbs have become popular neighborhood destinations. In addition, a variety of online booksellers, particularly specialty services, remain viable businesses, including many publishers who offer their backlist titles online directly to end-users, sometimes exclusively by making these titles unavailable to third-party distributors.

Printed books and newspapers have been disrupted by digital equivalents, but not eliminated. Whereas video rentals exist only as a footnote in the history of media, print is still alive and well. In fact, even though e-books, in the form of digital downloads on handheld devices or personal computers, may represent a faster-growing market category than printed books, print is still growing. Online distribution has accelerated the growth of printed books, especially with same- or two-day delivery. Newspapers, on the other hand, have been on a different trajectory. Printed newspapers, which have been in decline for the past decade, may eventually disappear.

As we all know from our own experiences with what has been a global standard for communicating news, many newspapers have folded for good or in some cases found a second life in a digital format. (For the most part, only fish-and-chips shops retain a vested interest in day-old newspapers.) But for a variety of compelling reasons—including ease of use, relative low cost, collectability, durability, shareability, and aesthetic appeal—printed books will likely be with us for some time to come. Still, the widespread usage of digital technology in all sectors of publishing has given birth to many more opportunities for both print and digital publishers to find additional revenue streams by responding to the shifting demands of their traditional customers, opening new markets, and publishing in more than a single medium.

The benefits of disruptive technology to consumers and producers of content alike are a recurring theme throughout the chapters of *Dealing with Disruption*. The dramatic changes in how published works are produced, distributed, and accessed by consumers enabled publishers to reach larger and more diverse audiences than previously possible. Any downside to, or fallout from this disruption—whether it meant the obsolescence of some types of printed products, fewer distribution channels, or greater consolidation in the industry—has been mitigated not only by the development of better ways to produce books and other media, but also by providing consumers with easier and cheaper access to an unlimited amount of information and knowledge. Thanks to the technology-driven vendors in the publishing ecosystem, consumers have benefitted from the convenience, functionality, and lower cost of digital books, newspapers, magazines, and journals and have gained easy access to previously hard-to-find or out-of-print publications—the so-called long tail.[1]

During the five years since the publication of *Dealing with Disruption*, we have seen continual, incremental change in the publishing industry, especially with the growth of interactive Web-based platforms that serve as gateways to a vast amount of cloud-based content. As a result, the business of digital publishing has become more complex and competitive. With the availability of a variety of content categories on a plethora of digital platforms, publishers have the additional challenge of cutting through an overwhelming amount of digital noise. Building awareness, creating customer loyalty, and demonstrating long-term value to an increasingly distracted market require a highly differentiated product plan as well as especially targeted marketing.

When I started my publishing career in the late 1970s, the end-to-end publishing process was tedious and time-consuming, and required many different resources to shepherd a manuscript from initial submission and acceptance to the finished product. Authors often submitted handwritten manuscripts; editors were thrilled if a manuscript had arrived typewritten. A marked-up manuscript by a copyeditor went to a compositor for typesetting, back to the publisher for page make-up, and back again to the compositor for corrections—printer's errors and additional editorial alterations. From this starting point, the manuscript embarked on a physical journey through the postal system as it traveled back and forth from the author to the publisher, then over to the compositor and ultimately to the printer before making its final trip to the distributor or retailer, or alternatively through the mail directly to the end-user. Shipping the manuscript through the various production steps to far-flung locations had an adverse effect on both publication schedules and development budgets.

Innovation in the production process has transformed manuscript preparation—reducing steps and costs, and increasing accuracy and speed to market. With current publishing software installed on a publisher's servers, or by using cloud-based applications, the manuscript does not move; it resides in cyberspace as various publishing professionals access it, at their convenience, in the same digital location, each performing their respective tasks to finalize a file before releasing it—instantly—to the printer for manufacturing in book form or to a website for digital downloads. The cost of mailing manuscripts and proofs from one stage to another need no longer be a line item on a publisher's profit and loss statement.

Publishing has come a long way since the invention of the printing press nearly 600 years ago. However, the lion's share of progress has occurred only in the past 25 years, starting with the first generation of digital technology. For most of the past six centuries, innovation has focused on incremental improvements in the printing press and binding operations, not on efficiencies in the development or distribution processes, or in added value or convenience for the consumer. Based on the speed with which technology causes change, and the successes that technology has had in almost every field of human endeavor, we should assume that we are only at the beginning stage of a publishing revolution; we should expect to experience and be part of even more dramatic change in the next 25 years.

As publishing evolves to adopt and utilize new digital tools in a progressively technology-driven marketplace, one of the biggest challenges for publishers will be identifying the right channels and business models for meeting consumer needs and growing market share. Currently, publishers must choose among a variety of options available and determine the most promising ones depending on the nature of the content and the expectation of consumers, who have become accustomed to accessing information in a variety of formats and at continually lower costs—whether they purchase, borrow, rent, or subscribe to a published work—and sometimes at no cost to them at all. Options are likely to increase in the future, and publishers must be able to adapt their business models accordingly.

In *Publishing in the Digital Age: How Business Can Thrive in a Rapidly Changing Environment*, I examine the various options available today in the publishing industry, including: Innovative product and data-driven marketing strategies that engage the contemporary knowledge seeker; methods for authors to gain agency over their work and find their audience without geographic limitations; and business models that enable publishers to respond to consumers' individual preferences.

The overarching theme of this book positions the publisher as a dynamic, innovative curator of information and knowledge, a creative force at the center of intersecting technologies—some that have stood the test of time and others that are still evolving. The supporting topics around this theme illustrate how publishers can:

- Use traditional and ground-breaking technologies to develop products in a variety of formats.
- Develop product and marketing strategies that expand and engage their customer base, increasing customer lifetime value.
- Prioritize collaboration with international partners to exploit a global market.

***

I could not have written this book without the expert assistance of generous colleagues who have given me invaluable insights from their own experiences with periodic shifts in digital technology as publishers and marketers from the United States, United Kingdom, India, and the Middle East. Their successes and challenges in producing, marketing, and distributing products in all formats and in diverse markets have helped me frame my own experiences within a broader context to provide practical strategies relevant to anyone engaged in the publishing business.

My gratitude goes out to: Vicki Smith Bigham, education product development, training, and marketing consultant, U.S.; Catherine Bruzzone, author, translator, and Founder of b small publishing, U.K.; Betsy Cohen, Executive Director, Youth Communications, U.S.; David Collins, Principal, Verulam Publishing Ltd., U.K.; Rachelle Cracchiolo, Founder & CEO, Teacher Created Materials, U.S.; Tim Ditlow, VP, Content, Epic, U.S.; Ian Grant, Partner, Creative Structure, Ltd., U.K.; Phyllis H. Hillwig, CEO and Founder of Math All Around and Eurekii, U.S.; Sam Hutchinson, Managing Director, b small publishing, U.K.; Peggy Intrator, Principal, Intrator Associates International Publishing Consultancy, U.S.; Mimi Jett, Co-Founder and CEO, Diglossia, U.A.E., U.S.; Dushyant Mehta, Chairman/CEO, Quadrum Solutions and Director, Repro India Ltd; Lynelle Morganthaler, VP Learning Design, Edmentum, U.S.; Ruth Pickering, Co-Founder & COO, Yewno, U.S.; Victor Rivero, Editor-in-Chief, EdTech Digest, U.S.; Marshall Ross, Vice Chairman/Chief Creative Officer, Cramer-Krasselt, U.S.; Dr. Merrick Ross, Professor of Surgical Oncology, M.D. Anderson Cancer Center, U.S.; Andrew Schlessinger, CEO & Co-Founder, SAFARI Montage, U.S.; Lisa Schmucki, Founder & CEO, EdWeb.net, U.S.; Amit Shah, Founder and Managing Director, Green Comma, U.S.; Ian Singer, CEO, LibraryPass, U.S.; Bill Smith, Publisher, BiographyPartner, U.S.; Jane Wightwick, author, translator, and Founder of Gaafar & Wightwick, U.K.

I would also like to thank you, the reader, for devoting your time to this book. I hope you find it useful in your work and your relationships with your colleagues. I would love to have your feedback and look forward to an ongoing conversation about publishing, education, and knowledge acquisition—and how we all can advance accuracy and truth in our daily lives. Be sure to let me know if something I have said is not clear, or if I have made any errors, big or small. I am sure there are some, and for that I apologize. I can be reached at: michael@michaelnross.com, or via my website, Ross & Associates, https://michaelnross.com.

Note

1 A concept coined by Chris Anderson in his book *The Long Tail: Why the Future of Business Is Selling Less of More*.

INTRODUCTION

Our analog past

> Knowledge is of two kinds. We know a subject ourselves, or we know where we can find information on it.
>
> —**Samuel Johnson**

Students of my generation, who attended U.S. elementary and secondary schools in the late 1950s and 1960s, had limited options for receiving information and acquiring knowledge. This was not due to cultural, social, or political barriers interfering with the publication of certain kinds of information. We were never concerned about state censorship, living as we did in a society where the First Amendment to the Constitution guaranteed the unimpeded flow of information and established freedom of speech and the press (two of the five immutable tenets of the First Amendment) the law of the land. Just like the previous generation and the generation before that, our access to current, curated, and timely information was not deterred by ideological constraints, but rather by the limits of the available technology and the logistical challenges associated with the distribution of intellectual property in physical form.

DOI: 10.4324/9781003162636-1

Content producers, writers, and editors were, at best, equipped with electric typewriters, the most advanced "word processing" tool from the 1960s through the mid-1980s. The standard for typesetting output was evolving from hot metal to phototypesetting, but personal computers, desktop publishing software, and digital printing technology stood far outside of our imagination. We had not taken even the first step on the path from knowledge scarcity to information overload. We lacked prolific, reliable, and steady means to learn about people and places, either in our neighborhoods or around the world, or to acquire accurate, updated information on a broad spectrum of intellectual pursuits. Our learning environment had more in common with the 19th century than the final years of the 20th century, even though the digital revolution—which would transform the publishing industry and provide easy access to more information than we could possibly absorb on any given day—was less than 35 years in the future.

Numbers and words, people and places

Apart from in-person get-togethers, telephony—consisting of fixed-line, or landline telephones—served as our primary means of communication.[1] Mostly everyone had a phone line.[2] To locate people or a business through their phone number, we relied on regional telephone directories—heavy, bulky, soft-cover books of millions of entries printed on thousands of thin sheets of paper and delivered free to homes and offices—which were commissioned by the telephone companies and supported by advertising revenue. Printed telephone directories in one form or another had been widely available—greatly increasing in size as the population grew—for more than 75 years.[3] The compilation, printing, and distribution of these directories quickly grew into a lucrative perennial business, and an important source of recurring revenue for the entire supply chain, especially the paper mills and printers who successfully negotiated multiyear contracts with the phone companies.

Consisting of "white pages" for residences and "yellow pages" for businesses, the massive phone directories, published annually, provided comprehensive A–Z listings of all phone subscribers for a specific region, which could be a single, large state or a consortium of smaller states. The organizational structure of the yellow pages—with alphabetically arranged listings within business and governmental categories—not only made it easy for users to narrow their search to pinpoint what they were looking for, it also incentivized businesses to trade under a moniker that might help them be more easily discovered among the thousands of entries and perhaps hundreds of competitors in their industry. A plumber, for example, might choose to trade under the name "A-1 Plumbing" so that it would appear at the top of the plumbing listings. Another vendor might be called "AA-1 Plumbing" or "AAA-1 Plumbing" to rank even higher. "Zach Zappa's Plumbing and Pipe Fitting" would likely end up at the bottom of the list unless Mr. Zappa had the foresight to put the initial "A" in front of his first name. A lower position among the listings would likely reduce the "traffic" to the company's entry, which could mean fewer customers and less revenue.

In an analog world, this alpha-numerical naming convention had practical marketing value, especially among small, local businesses; if potential customers did not know a plumber or electrician to call, for example, and had not received recommendations from a friend or neighbor, they would consult the yellow pages and most likely pick one of the first few names on the list. Marketers and brand managers were cognizant of this natural user behavior, which led to a "land grab" by businesses to use "As" and "1s" at the start of their names.

In a way, the scramble for names that had the potential to rise to the top of the alphabetical listings was the analog version of "search engine optimization," or the equivalent of the tactics that digital marketers use today to climb to the top-ranking position of search results pages by purchasing keywords or adding subject-relevant content to their websites, in addition to making ad buys. A multibillion-dollar industry has developed around strategies that help websites occupy a place on the first page of a search. Businesses would also buy ads in the yellow pages to capture users' attention. Given the limitations of the print format, you had two choices to stand out among your competitors: You could buy the largest ad on the page or decorate your message with catchy graphics, but neither compares to the sophistication needed to prompt search engine algorithms to favor your website and hopefully propel it to the first page of the search results.

Remarkably, this naming convention persists today, even though having a company name that starts with "AAA-1 this" or "A&A that" has no practical value in a digital world. Why there are still so many companies with names like this—from contractors, landscapers, and pest exterminators to appliance centers, carpet cleaners, and landscapers—is probably something of a mystery to members of the digital-native generation who have never used the yellow pages.

I have reproduced here a short excerpt (abbreviated to eliminate redundant entries and with the actual phone numbers edited) from the first page of the business section of the online version of my local yellow pages, listing disparate companies alphabetically regardless of category. The last entry in the listing, "A American Custom Flooring," is not a typo, but probably an attempt to differentiate the company from all of the companies that start with "American," as well as to achieve a top spot among flooring specialists. One really must admire the mastermind who came up with the "A AAAABA Escort Service." In addition to striving to occupy the highest position within the escort service category, a secondary goal may have been to make the name almost impossible to remember, under the assumption that the service would not be used more than once.

Phone books continued to land on doorsteps long after they became obsolete. But even several years before the last of these dinosaurs was printed in 2017, most of the directories delivered to homes and businesses went directly from the front door to the recycling bin with the cellophane wrapping still intact.[4]

Regional yellow pages today have new lives as websites, but

A A A Garage Door Repair
2100 Green Bay Rd Evnstn ------------------ 555 448-1556
A A A Northwest Vacuum Cleaners
7042 W Higgins Av Chgo ------------------ 500 300-8227
A A A Sure Plumbing ------------------ 500 499-9146
A & A Accredited Alcohol & Drug Detox Rehab Treatment Center For Recov Derfld ------- 555 607-0713
A & A Drug Rehab & Alcohol Detox Treatment Center 24 Hour Helpline Glenvw ---------- 555 730-2200
A A Drug Rehab & Oxycontin-Vicodin Detox Treatment Park Ridge ------------------ 555 728-9996
AAA Alarm Systems Inc NILES ------------- 555 966-5494
AAA Appliances Service Center
416 Higgins Rd Park Ridge ------------------ 555 823-6000
AAA Auto Club 126 Skokie Blvd Skokie ---- 555 679-8706
AAA Enterprises 1155 Hartrey Av Evnstn -- 500 303-1784
AAA Painting Contractors Inc
30W 640 North Av W Chgo ------------------ 500 450-5219
AAA Roadside Service of Park Ridge
1598 W Marcus Ct Park Ridge -------------- 555 653-0013
AAA Travel Agency ---------------------- 555 364-4645
A AAAABA Escort Service
Chicago Morton Grove TelNo ---------------- 555 967-0670
A-Adams School of Driving Inc
6040 Dempster St Morton Grove ------------ 555 965-6565
A & A Alcohol Abuse & Drug Addiction Treatment Center 24 Hour Helpline Park Ridge ------- 555 720-3998
A American Custom Flooring
7777 N Caldwell Niles --------------------- 555 966-0500

for finding a specific business quickly or discovering a business within a designated category, they cannot compete with results generated from a search engine. Still, occasions may arise when it might be useful to see at a glance an entire category's listings, a commonly utilized rubric that the first Internet search engines adopted to make their sites as intuitive as possible to users already familiar with the organizational structure of print directories.[5] If you want to know the entire list of businesses in a geographic area or even all the businesses within a particular service category, such as hair salons in New Jersey, you might want to check the online version of the yellow pages directory, which looks just like its print counterpart with a table of contents and businesses listed alphabetically by type. It may not be as efficient as entering "hair salons" in a search box, but it might be an option for anyone who prefers browsing to searching.

Given their weight, bulk, and design, phone books were a cumbersome, wasteful, and ultimately inadequate solution to the challenge of providing the public with a comprehensive and practical list of phone numbers. Phone books contained both too much information and not enough. If you lived in California, which in 1960 had a population of 16 million, the statewide directory that you received from the phone company contained millions of phone numbers and thousands of pages of data that would probably be of no use to you. To gain access to the relatively small subset of telephone numbers that you might occasionally need, you had no other choice but to keep a four-inch-thick tome, weighing around four pounds, on your shelf or in a cupboard. At the same time, if you needed a phone number for someone in the neighboring state of Nevada, you were out of luck unless you were visiting there and could locate a local phone directory. Regardless of where you lived, it would not be practical to own a stack of phone books from all or even some of the other states just to have access to the few numbers that you might need at some point in the future. An expensive option would be to call a live operator, which was the only way to reach a number in another country; rather than a convenience, however, this service was a forced dependency brought about by a handicapped solution to a problem, as well as an added cost to the phone companies that provided the service. Today, the standard marketing response would be to call this product deficiency a "feature." Today, with an almost unlimited quantity of information available in the cloud, we do not need to have a library of books in our house to find most of the so-called "look-up" information we may need.

As a characteristic of print products with excessively large data sets like phone directories, giving consumers more information than they would ever need (and not enough of what they did need), was a decades-long problem waiting for a solution, and not unique to telephone directories. The venerable 20-volume *Oxford English Dictionary*, for example, while arguably containing indispensable, scholarly knowledge, was a flawed product in print and, from a user's point of view, can be most appreciated in a digital format and accessed on the Web. The editors of the OED set out to create "the definitive record of the English language" from A to Z, which took the form of a multivolume set of books with more than 500,000 words and their definitions, including their derivations and usage over time. For most owners of the set of books, many of the volumes on their shelves would never be opened, which meant that they were paying a steep price for each word they looked up when measured against the fixed cost of the entire set, not to mention the amount of shelf space that was required. Asking consumers to pay for more volumes than they needed was a marketing hurdle; but arguably a more problematic obstacle to overcome was the OED's extenuated publication schedule from its debut in 1888, whereby the volumes were slowly released a letter or two every couple of years.[6] In 1971, the OED was issued in a giant two-volume "Compact Edition," with four photographically reduced pages of the full-sized OED printed on each of the more than 4,000 pages. The set came with a magnifying glass to make the tiny print almost readable. It certainly took up less shelf space and was more affordable, but it created its own barrier to entry.

Many data-heavy publications like the OED transitioned from print to CD-ROMs when that technology became available. The CD-ROM discs had many advantages over the printed volumes; given the amount of content they could store, they took up extraordinarily little space, cost much less, did not require the harvesting of trees, and offered benefits not feasible with print, like multimedia content, hyperlinks, search capability, and interactivity. But not everyone had personal computers when CD-ROMs were first introduced, and ultimately CD-ROMs and their more capacious cousins, DVD-ROMs, became a bridge technology to product websites and apps, which had the further advantage of being continually up to date, more accurate and economical, and device agnostic.

The phone companies did not transition to CD-ROMs, and until the Internet became commonplace, continued to update, and print, directories every year. Even if the phone companies and their partners in the publishing process could have found a more efficient way to get phone numbers into the hands of their subscriber base, they were not motivated to do so because producing the directories was a successful business with benefits for all participants—with advertising revenue for the phone companies; brand awareness, and customer acquisition opportunities for the ad buyers; and recurring, multiyear contracts for the printers and paper mills. Despite the unwieldy nature of the phone books and their inherent deficiencies, consumers happily used them because there were no alternatives, and they were free.

Prior to the emergence of digital publishing, the development of some types of products and the mechanisms for rolling them out to the market occasionally created unorthodox alliances in the supply chain, which affected how a product was designed, what features it had, and how it was packaged and delivered. The supply chain in publishing has always brought together entities with different priorities, risks, cost structures, and customers. Some early relationship models demonstrate how unexpected relationships can sometimes play key roles in the development and distribution of new products. Even though the publication of telephone directories generated substantial revenue for the phone companies, printers, and paper mills for decades, it is unlikely that as a technology company, whose core competency was delivering reliable phone service, the phone companies intended or really wanted to be both a publisher and a distributor of print products. But getting as many people as possible to use their phones was an important goal and supplying directories of every phone number in their system to their entire subscriber base was a logical way to accomplish that. In addition, advertising unlocked a new revenue stream and enabled them to deliver directories to consumers at no charge.

The free directory service provided by the phone companies can be viewed as a precursor to the model that search engines and social media platforms use today. Technology companies like Google and Facebook, for example, get most of their revenue from advertising, which allows them to offer their search or communication services to consumers for free. But unlike the phone companies, they would not consider themselves publishers, but rather conduits, or platforms, for third-party content. By producing and delivering organized content, the phone companies became de facto publishers and distributors, roles they assumed for decades until the Internet enabled a much more efficient service without wasting paper or staffing an army of human operators.

Just as telephone directories served as our primary source for finding people, similarly, we used physical maps to locate man-made or natural places like towns, rivers, lakes, and parks, and to find the best routes from one destination to another. To get to these places, most of us relied on buses or cars and an inchoate but expanding road and highway system. The U.S. roadway and highway infrastructure received an injection of resources from the government with the passage of two bills, the Federal Aid Road Act of 1916, and the Federal Aid Highway Act of 1921, which prioritized the construction of a national road grid.[7] These initiatives motivated the oil industry to devise ways to encourage Americans to spend more time on the road to increase their consumption of gasoline. As it turned out, the largest U.S. mapmaker at the time, Rand McNally, which had been developing cartographic products since the late 19th century, was also instrumental in creating a system for numbering the roads, which was ultimately adopted by state and federal highway authorities. This led to a partnership between the oil industry and Rand McNally to use the latter's maps to encourage people to travel more on the roads by making driving safer and easier, resulting in increased spending on gasoline and a direct benefit to the oil industry's bottom line.

When Rand McNally launched their road maps in 1920, the Gulf Oil Company's network of service stations became their exclusive distribution channel. This relationship between the largest U.S. map publisher and gasoline stations around the country is legendary. Rand McNally road maps were ubiquitous in the specially designed racks and kiosks at these pit stops along the sides of U.S. roads and highways for more than eight decades. It is also likely that this distribution relationship, and the use of maps primarily by automobile travelers and truck drivers, is major inducement behind the form factor of the many-sided road maps, which I have always found nearly impossible to unfold and refold the same way twice.[8]

Rand McNally's dominance in road map publishing may have begun with this unique distribution arrangement with an oil company, but for almost the entire 20th century, they remained the most recognized brand in cartographic publications and products. On the road, at homes, or in schools, if you sought geographic information of any kind, you more than likely turned to a Rand McNally map, atlas, or globe. Over the years, they expanded to produce best-selling atlases, specialty maps, and travel guidebooks, and at one point opened retail stores specializing in travel-related books and gear. At their peak, and before digital cartography took over, a Rand McNally wall map was in nearly every classroom in the country, and various editions of their school world atlas, which was first published in 1923, remained the standard reference for accurate information for high school social studies and college geography courses for decades.

Rand McNally began creating digital maps in 1982 and issued a fully digital road atlas in 1993, but by the mid-1990s, they had lost their grip on the direction and speed with which the cartography business had been heading and ceded the innovation of digital cartography to technology companies like MapQuest. GPS systems on handheld devices and later mobile phones were making the printed road maps, the largest source of revenue for the company, obsolete. As other technology companies like Google and Apple took over the mapping space, Rand began to lose their status as the premier brand for maps and atlases for which they were synonymous for more than a century. Today, cartographic books, like atlases and folded maps, once a major source of information as well as a substantial publishing category, have been almost entirely replaced by digital alternatives.

Knowledge most worth owning

Mid-20th-century classrooms had not changed much over the preceding 100 years. If, hypothetically, students from 19th-century London were transported to a Chicago classroom in the 20th century, the surroundings would most likely feel remarkably familiar, with a teacher in front of a blackboard, printed textbooks on undersized desks, and notebooks with pens and pencils for taking quizzes and doing homework.

The consumption of information was accomplished through the narrow delivery funnels of print and, to some extent, analog broadcast media, which offered a paucity of choices. If we wanted to know, read, or learn about something, we had to buy a newspaper or magazine, borrow books from the library, or tune in to one of just a small number of radio or television channels. The opportunities to purchase books were few and far between; in fact, I do not remember buying any books until college, which roughly coincided with the opening of the first Barnes and Noble bookshop in 1971. As they do today, grocery stores sold an assortment of books, and occasionally promoted a multivolume encyclopedia in the form of a "continuity series"—one alphabetized volume at a time over a period of many months. This may have been an inexpensive way to acquire a reference work, but the purchasing model had an obvious handicap for even the most patient buyer: If you started collecting the books and had secured only volumes "A" through "O" when you had a paper due on, say, "the planets," you were out of luck.[9]

Book-of-the-month clubs mailed books to homes on a subscription basis, but the titles were generally on mass-market subjects or popular fiction. Time-Life Books, where I got my first job in publishing after graduate school, was a popular mail-order publisher that regularly released several series of multivolume hardbound sets of books on general-interest topics like "Photography," "The Enchanted World," "Mysteries of the Unknown," "Myth and Mankind," and "The Old West." Although they were professionally researched and written, beautifully illustrated and manufactured with attractive, durable bindings, they did not align to the curriculum and consequently were of little use for schoolwork. The editors of Time-Life Books did not take academic subjects into consideration when choosing, organizing, and packaging the content. When we needed informational books, or primary sources, that explored curricular topics in more detail than the summary presentations in textbooks and that could help with our homework assignments, we had to visit our school or local public library.

Still, Time-Life Books sold an impressive number of books directly to consumers from 1957 until their demise in 2001, reaching a peak of 30 million books a year. The editorial direction and marketing strategy behind it ultimately contributed to their downfall. The original publisher, Jerome Hardy, thought that they would thrill their customers by creating a series of titles on a broad range of topics consisting of an entire shelf full of volumes each, sometimes more than 30 books on a single topic, giving "the customer more than he has any right to expect." This marketing scheme might have been viewed in a favorable light if the consumer didn't have to pay for the "extra" content.[10] Giving consumers more than they needed, wanted, or "had any right to expect"—which now seems like a presumptuous proposition, at a minimum—meant that the publisher had to continuously produce and send out additional volumes to a number of published sets already taking up substantial shelf space in the subscribers' homes. At some point, buyers would conclude that they probably did not need volume 25 of, say, "The Old West," or all 33 volumes of "Mysteries of the Unknown"; how many unknown mysteries does the average person really need to know about? Today, if you have an online subscription to a reference work, large database, or streaming service, you pay a fixed fee that you have determined provides good value based on how much you use and how well you judged the experience. The service increases in value as the publisher or distributor adds more content that you continue to appreciate. Netflix, HBO, and Disney Plus are good examples of how a value-based entertainment subscription model works; the OED online is a similar kind of model assessed in the same way if you are a knowledge worker or word lover, as is Westlaw online if you are a lawyer. A publishing model whose value proposition exceeded customer expectations was difficult to achieve in the analog era of publishing.

Forecasting the inventory needs of the later volumes in a thematic series was an additional problem that the publisher faced with this kind of print subscription model. Since a subscriber typically would have to commit to only the first few volumes in the series and not the entire series up front, the publisher did not have adequate data to determine the ultimate demand of a series and how many volumes of the entire set it should print, which often resulted in excess inventory on most sets that numbered more than two or three volumes. Unlike an encyclopedia, thematically structured sets might not seem to have a logical end. So, losing customers somewhere in the middle of their subscription term meant that the publisher would receive less revenue than forecast and would end up with additional inventory and storage costs for books in a series that had been printed but not sold. The excess inventory would have to be remaindered or destroyed. We referred to this languishing stock as "brown bananas." Thus, "give the customer more than he has any right to expect" not only sounds much better than it is, but it failed in creating long-term customer value. With digital products, customers pay a fixed price for options that they can see are available at any given moment, and the price stays fixed even as the options and the value of the subscription increase over time.

Paper thin and bound to end

To acquire general knowledge, read about the lives of great men and women of history, and explore topics like the universe, philosophy, mathematics, science, and the arts, students relied on one of several multivolume encyclopedias that were ubiquitous from the 1950s through the early 1990s. Although these five decades could be regarded as the heyday of multivolume encyclopedias, some version of an encyclopedia had been the primary source of general knowledge—literally from A to Z—since the 18th century with the publication of the three-volume Britannica. First printed in 1768 in Edinburgh by "a society of gentlemen in Scotland,"[11] the Britannica continued to expand over the next 150 years but was available mostly to an elite, scholarly British audience. During World War I, the Britannica was purchased by the American mail-order company Sears, Roebuck, which, over time, increased the number of volumes by adding thousands of simplified articles to make the encyclopedia more accessible to a broader audience. Several other encyclopedia publishers jockeyed for market share during this same period; however, the Britannica's main competitor was the World Book Encyclopedia, which was first published in 1917, around the time when the Britannica was brought to America. Coincidentally, they both established their headquarters in Chicago.

The companies that published these two encyclopedias targeted different segments of the market. The Britannica, staying true to its Scottish roots, was regarded as the more scholarly reference publication, renowned for the caliber of its contributors—including Nobel Prize winners—and its literary style, which appealed to advanced secondary school and university students, academics, and researchers. In its final format of 32 small-print, sturdily bound volumes of approximately 1,000 three-column pages each, the Britannica would have the distinction of becoming the oldest continuously published reference work in the English language. The World Book, with the marketing slogan "Organized Knowledge in Story and Picture,"[12] was geared to a younger audience, primarily ages 14 and up; had a more user-friendly layout; boasted more illustrations, many in color; and included research tips and article outlines to help students write their homework assignments. With only 22 volumes in its largest configuration, it could be shipped in a single carton, instead of Britannica's three, took up less space on the shelf, and cost less. The World Book relinquished the top tier of the market to the Britannica, but reached a broader audience, making it more popular and outselling the Britannica by about three to one.[13]

By the mid-1960s, through aggressive advertising campaigns and strong sales results, the Britannica and World Book had become household names, and the companies that produced them grew into publishing juggernauts, eventually reaching millions of homes and public libraries around the world—with substantial market penetration in North America, the United Kingdom, Ireland, Australia, South Africa, India, and the Philippines—including law firms, corporate libraries, and, especially in the case of the Britannica, diplomatic bureaus and embassies, where a bookcase of the venerable reference set was considered a hallmark of scholarship and prestige.

Encyclopedias thrived as they afforded their owners the only available gateway to a world of knowledge at one's fingertips—not with a click of the mouse but from thousands of pages on a shelf. As the English-speaking world's must-have reference work for what the early-20th-century Britannica company advertised as "the sum of human knowledge," the encyclopedia served as the "Internet" of its time.[14] Given the resources required to edit, compile, print, and pack thousands of encyclopedia sets each year, and ship them from a U.S. Midwest printer on roads, rail, or water to homes, schools, and libraries around the globe, the "era of the encyclopedia," which flourished for generations, may represent the most remarkable achievement in the history of print publishing.

From the vantage point of the 21st century, where information is no longer scarce or confined to a single medium, it's easy to see how vulnerable the encyclopedia business was, and why it was the first major publishing category to be disrupted significantly by digital technology, forcing encyclopedia publishers to abandon their primary revenue-generating product line, pivot to a digital platform, and completely change their marketing strategy to survive in any form at all. Compared with the demise of the video rental business, the collapse of the printed encyclopedia business is even more stunning given its 250-year history and role as the most authoritative source of information and knowledge for most of that time.[15]

Still, despite its place in history and decades of success, the encyclopedia business, even at the apex of its market penetration and influence, was better at generating profits for the publishing companies and their printing partners than at giving customers the products that displayed the value that they expected. The development and manufacturing tools available to publishers equipped them with the means to build a robust business—creating jobs for hundreds of editors and thousands of sales representatives[16]—but not make an entirely adequate consumer product that could deliver on its ambitious promise. Looking at how the printed encyclopedias evolved over time, one would conclude that the publishers did their best to address consumer needs and produce authoritative and accessible products at the highest possible editorial and manufacturing standards. However, limited to a finite number of printed volumes and an annual printing cycle, they ultimately could not realize their objectives to be both comprehensive (comprising "the sum of human knowledge") and current—accurate, relevant, and always up to date. These lofty goals were not achievable with a fiscally responsible number of human resources working in a print-only environment.

When selecting and editing articles for encyclopedias, editors had two primary objectives in mind: To set aside their biases as best they could to provide the information and knowledge "most worth having"; and to ensure that the information they included was as up to date as possible. However, they had only so much space for new articles and limited resources to revise aging and outdated articles. They could not continue to add an unlimited number of volumes as information and knowledge grew, nor could they make changes in their product and deliver updated information to their customers on a real-time basis.

Ideally, the content was meant to meet the needs of every reader regardless of where they lived and what their interests might be. But since it would not be practical to manufacture multiple versions of an extensive multi-volume encyclopedia, editors were forced into a one-size-fits-all strategy, which produced a database that was bound to fall short of the expectations of many thousands of readers. Students in, say, Sydney, Australia and Atlanta, Georgia probably would not be equally interested in the causes of the American Civil War. Likewise, encyclopedia owners in Manchester, England and Manila, Philippines would not have the same compulsion to study the history of the British monarchy.

Even as more volumes were added to include new and revised entries to meet the needs of a broader global market, there was a limit to how large the encyclopedias could become, and therefore, how much content they could eventually contain. First, editorial capacity limited how many articles from the thousands of contributing authors could be managed and how much updating could be undertaken. Second, manufacturing costs had to be managed: The more volumes an encyclopedia contained, the more expensive the product would be for the end-user. *World Book* retained a price advantage over *Britannica* because it had fewer, and shorter, volumes. But it was also less comprehensive in scope and went into less detail on the same topics. Although, in theory, the publishers could periodically add volumes to the corpus, which both Britannica and World Book did over time, they had to manage the resources necessary to produce and maintain the content to minimize the effect of production costs on the final price of their products.

Balancing these financial objectives meant that, at some point, there had to be a fixed number of volumes in a set. Still, both the *Britannica* and *World Book* represented a major investment for families (and libraries) in their current configurations. Charge cards were still new to the consumer market in the 1950s and 1960s, so a family would typically pay for their set on an installment plan. To purchase the *Britannica*, for example, a family would pay about a third of what it would cost to buy a new Volkswagen Beetle.[17]

But the prospective rise in costs to the customer for additional volumes was not the only constraint facing the publishers. The delivery service, primarily UPS, that shipped the sets had established a strict weight limit on the boxes in which the books were packed. Both the *Britannica* and *World Book* had reached their maximum weight limits for their respective shipping cartons (three boxes for Britannica, one for World Book). Therefore, to keep the sets from exceeding their weight limits, the editors had to maintain a certain number of pages per volume as well as a firm number of volumes per set. These physical limitations strained editorial resources and directly affected the quality and quantity of the content.

To control page count, and ultimately the size and number of the volumes, the editors classified the content into tiers of perishability, making assumptions about how frequently articles on different topics would have to be updated. To the extent possible, the editors included entries that were mostly "evergreen"—i.e., that rarely needed to be updated, such as biographies of historical figures—and kept the more perishable content (country data, or listings of politicians, for example) to a minimum. Some articles were written with the expectation that they would stay current for ten years, others five years, some—the minority—one to two years. To manage the process, management established a team of editors dedicated to adding, revising, or simply removing articles. This activity was called "space patrol." If a new article needed to be added, or an existing article revised, chances were that something had to come out. Sometimes excellent content had to be deleted to make room for what the editors determined was more relevant content—all to ensure that the product did not exceed its weight limits. If there were no weight limits and, in turn, restrictions on the number of volumes in a set, many more articles would have stayed in the set and have been revised if necessary. This kind of constraint would not be a factor in a knowledge database developed, revised, and delivered on the Web, which would be liberating to content developers and a tangible benefit to users. Further, the additional cost of the editorial work required to maintain the size of the print encyclopedia ultimately had an impact on its final price. Even with the draconian effort it took to keep the encyclopedia as relevant and current as possible, some percentage of the content inevitably would be out of date as soon as the set went to press. Over time the entire encyclopedia would become dated and less reliable, aging like milk rather than wine.

Since making available as much relevant and up-to-date information as possible to their patrons is part of their mission, librarians often built the cost of buying a new encyclopedia every three or four years into their budgets, or they might buy a different encyclopedia on alternating years. A family, however, would typically buy only one encyclopedia and keep it for many years—long past the time when their children would make use of it—and therefore needed a way to keep their substantial investment up to date. Filling this requirement resulted in an excellent business opportunity for the publisher, but not a wholly satisfactory solution for the consumer. To provide new information and update existing content in the encyclopedias, the publishers created annual supplements called yearbooks.[18] The yearbooks were sold to encyclopedia owners as a vehicle for including articles about people, significant discoveries, or major political and cultural events that were not in the prior year's set, and a curated chronicle of current events that occurred during the past year. For the most part, encyclopedia owners purchased these "supplements" intending to keep their encyclopedias up to date and to protect their initial investment. Most bought into this strategy, which resulted in an excellent way for the publishers to gain additional revenue from their existing and growing customer base. Millions of encyclopedia supplements were printed and sold each year as more customers were added to the ranks of encyclopedia purchasers. In effect, the encyclopedias were the razors and the yearbooks the razor blades. In marketing terms, the yearbook would be considered an upsell, delivered to customers at the end of each year on a "negative-option" basis, meaning that as soon as they were published, the books were mailed to customers, who then had the "option" to either send the company a check to cover the cost of the book, plus shipping, or return it. Most customers found it easier to send in a check than to repack and mail back the book.[19]

Although the yearbooks contained new information and revisions to existing articles, they obviously did not *physically* update the printed encyclopedia. Year after year, encyclopedia owners would place their new yearbook on the shelf next to the last volume in their set and after the yearbook from the previous year; but without being thoroughly familiar with the contents of each supplement, users would not necessarily know which one to consult if they wanted the most up-to-date information on any given subject, making the yearbook an inadequate and inconvenient tool for what it was designed to do. If, for example, a family had bought an encyclopedia between 1922 and 1991, they would learn from the article on the Soviet Union that the U.S.S.R. was a one-party state. But by December 1991, the U.S.S.R. had broken up, which meant that all the articles about it in the sets from those past years were obsolete. In addition, all references to the Soviet Union throughout those sets would be dated. (Even encyclopedias with a 1992 copyright were most likely editorially closed and published too late to reflect the U.S.S.R.'s dissolution.) If a family had signed up to receive the yearbooks, they would have to know—and remember which year to consult—about the Soviet breakup and the newly formed independent countries. If the print encyclopedia were a computer system, we might consider the yearbook a kind of updating "hack." Yet because it was the only way to maintain their original investment as a continually updated product, millions of encyclopedia owners signed on to the annual supplement program and collected yearbooks for many years after their initial encyclopedia purchase. In some cases, the number of yearbooks a customer bought exceeded the number of volumes in their original set of encyclopedias.

I worked in the general reference and encyclopedia publishing business for 25 years, first as executive vice president and publisher for World Book, Inc., from 1992 to 2002, and then as the senior vice president for educational product development, marketing, and sales for Britannica, Inc., from 2002 until 2017. During that time, I saw the encyclopedia print business at Britannica go from a robust publishing enterprise to zero in 2013.[20] In the early 1990s, both companies were thoroughly invested in similar business strategies that revolved around selling a general-knowledge print encyclopedia, annual supplements, and a few supplemental thematic works of reference on specific topics like science and art and a range of children's series. They had also begun to develop digital products while still maintaining their print business, which was responsible for most of their revenue through the first few years of the 21st century.

By the mid-1990s, the rise of digital solutions for knowledge products hit like a tsunami, which had a dramatic impact on the sales of the print encyclopedia and caused the encyclopedia companies to re-examine their business models and accelerate their digital development efforts. There were several elements of the business model that needed reform. For starters, with print sales in rapid decline, the outside sales force had to be dismantled and marketing had to be repositioned to manage a digital product line with a much lower price point, a different breed of competitors, and a new network of distributors.

Early in the development of digital technologies, the management of both companies recognized that producing digital products, which at that time were mainly CD-ROMs (or DVDs), would allow the editorial teams to streamline their processes, eliminate length barriers on articles, greatly expand the database, and shorten the publishing cycle. By adding search capabilities and multimedia elements, editors could enhance the content, increase the educational value of the articles, and provide a much more engaging consumer experience. But to move forward with the new technology in earnest, they had to address the entrenched supply chain and the sales structure that had been responsible for the growth of their print products and brands over many decades.

The large sales forces that both World Book and Britannica had established, rewarded, and elevated over the decades clearly understood that they had no role to play in the selling of digital products that could be purchased through retail channels at a fraction of the cost of a set of books. Most were

INTRODUCTION   19

not interested in adapting to a new sales environment and instead fought hard to maintain their turf and tried to discourage the company from pursuing digital solutions that would replace the traditional print products and put their jobs at risk.

During my tenure at World Book, I was caught in the middle of spearheading the development of digital products while at the same time investing in enough enhancements to the print products to maintain some of the customer base and boost sales force morale. CD-ROM sales were still relatively small compared with the legacy print business, but print sales were declining as consumer appetite for the new technology products increased. We had to proceed on two fronts simultaneously—move rapidly, but with fiscal restraint, to a digital product profile, while at the same time continue to develop and expand the print business. This meant balancing two separate editorial processes, adding additional technology resources for the digital products, finding new distribution channels for CD-ROMs, and placating a direct sales force. Juggling these objectives made achieving success in any of them a challenge.

Customer demand for print continued to wane as more CD-ROM products in more categories became available. The trendlines were clear, and in the face of technology that could deliver large amounts of content-rich titles and more features at much lower prices, the print equivalents had few if any competitive advantages. The only selling advantage that print could claim would be for the segment of the customer base that did not have computers or had no intention of getting them. An encyclopedia on CD-ROM also demonstrated that the standard, iconic A–Z organization was a print-centric convenience only and not a value-add for the consumer. If they had a choice, readers would not likely be interested following topics solely because they appeared next to each other in the alphabet, or in the same lettered volume. The CD-ROM search made this organization obsolete. An argument could be made for browsing and learning about topics that you had not considered. But random topics in a single volume does not make for an enjoyable cover-to-cover read. Sometimes the juxtaposition of articles that share proximity in the alphabet in the same volume produces comical results, like the first and last entries of Volume Eight in the *Britannica* (wording on the spine is shown on the left), which (and I cannot resist the pun) make for odd bedfellows.

| 8 |
| MENAGE |
| OTTAWA |

By the late 1990s, the outside sales force had shrunk considerably, and the remaining representatives focused their efforts mostly on library sales; but even in that loyal print market, the sales force ran into resistance with mounting user preference for digital reference products that provided more value at lower costs and did not occupy valuable shelf space.

As the millennium approached, the World Book sales force was desperate for something new that would help them keep the status quo and to preserve their livelihoods. We had little room to innovate within the context of a print encyclopedia beyond what had already been done with illustrations, maps, and transparent overlays; and none of these visual elements could compete with the multimedia and interactivities on a CD-ROM.

To create excitement that would be unique to the print format, and not possible to accomplish with a CD-ROM, we looked to the physical dimensions of the set—the real estate it occupied, how it appeared on a shelf—and re-imagined the facing columns of spines as a blank canvas. Working with my veteran art director, I introduced the concept of using a single visual image, or visual theme, that would span the spines of the 2000 "Millennium Edition," which could be seen even from the full length of a classroom. The art director and I selected a photo of a "sunrise"—as a tribute to the dawn of a new millennium.[21] I called this visual presentation a "spinescape," which World Book ultimately trademarked and continued to implement as a motif, with a different image for every subsequent annual edition. Although the spinescape was an interesting novelty, it did little to curb the decline in sales; it may have looked more compelling than the traditional monochrome design, but it added no value to the customer looking for information on a specific topic.

While the traditional encyclopedia companies were struggling with their sales forces in denial, and simultaneously repositioning their businesses for the digital future, competitors stepped in and captured the mindshare and market share of the digital encyclopedia market out from under them. The main competitor was *Encarta*, a multimedia encyclopedia on CD-ROM that Microsoft built from a licensed version of the *Funk & Wagnall's New Encyclopedia*, best known as a supermarket encyclopedia for its historical distribution channel. Microsoft also plundered the editorial ranks of World Book and Britannica, brought an experienced team of encyclopedia developers to their headquarters in Redmond, WA, and upgraded the *Funk & Wagnall's* into a viable editorial product. At the same time, Microsoft had all the technology and design muscle it needed to make *Encarta* a first-rate technology product that stood out primarily for its bells and whistles, which made up for any weaknesses in the depth and breadth of the content.

At its launch, *Encarta* was sold in computer retail stores for under $100 but was primarily bundled free with computers. Since PC's were relatively new on the market, the PC makers were looking for ways to demonstrate the "need, use, and value" of PCs for individual users. As it turned out, an encyclopedia on a CD-ROM was the perfect product to demonstrate the reason for owning a computer, since an entire print set could be contained on one disc, at a fraction of the cost, or even free, with the added benefit of many more articles, videos, and animations. Microsoft's main corporate mission was "a computer on every desk and in every home," which meant that promoting their Windows operating system, the software engine behind most PCs, was paramount.[22]

Microsoft developed *Encarta* for the primary purpose of getting as many Windows-based computers on the market as possible, not to produce the best encyclopedia or even to take market share away from other encyclopedia companies. But that is exactly what happened. Getting a CD-ROM encyclopedia free with a computer purchase, where the alternative was paying nearly $2,000 for a print set or paying for a more expensive CD-ROM from World Book or Britannica, was a tremendous value proposition for the new PC buyer. Although the content of Microsoft's *Encarta* was not on par with the *Britannica*, or the *World Book*, the market preferred both the price and the technology advantages of the *Encarta* over any authoritative advantage that the premier brands might have. Neither World Book nor Britannica had a chance against a competitor that was willing to invest millions of dollars in a product that they gave away for free or at a huge discount. Microsoft used *Encarta* as a trojan horse to dominate the PC market and make Windows the most popular operating system on the planet; disrupting the traditional encyclopedia business was simply collateral damage.

With their enthusiasm for the new technology, consumers were sending the encyclopedia makers a message—that that they cared more about the bells and whistles in the new technology, and the much lower price, than they did about the quality of the content or the brand. Apparently, the venerable *Britannica* on CD-ROM, with star authors like Harry Houdini, Albert Einstein, Marie Curie, Sigmund Freud, Henry Ford, Leon Trotsky; U.S. presidents John F. Kennedy, Jimmy Carter, Bill Clinton; Madeleine Albright,

Archbishop Desmond Tutu, and Martin Scorsese, was not as compelling as a souped-up *Funk & Wagnall's* as long as it was free or cheap.

Having a multimedia CD-ROM bundled as part of their PC purchase not only motivated the buyer to purchase the PC, but it also reduced the value of all other CD-ROM encyclopedias, including the premier brands. Microsoft's use of *Encarta* to increase its penetration of Windows OS was not unlike the strategy that the oil companies used to increase the sales of gasoline by distributing road maps. Proof that this was their strategy was that not long after the CD-ROMs or DVDs were discontinued and then converted to a website, *Encarta* was taken off the market.[23]

While losing brand appeal in the CD-ROM wars was a problem for both World Book and Britannica, going online revealed other vulnerabilities. The restrictions that governed the production of their legacy print products left both companies with databases that were too small to meet the needs of users of the Internet, where the expectation was to get a result for every attempted search. In 2001, *Wikipedia*, the first encyclopedia born on the Internet, was launched with around 1,000 articles. *Wikipedia*, free to consumers and with no advertising, was designed as crowd-sourced, non-profit project that allowed anyone to contribute or edit. From a slow start, the database grew quickly and in many languages. Today, the English edition of *Wikipedia* contains approximately 6.2 million articles, which would be the equivalent to around 2,800 print volumes of the *Encyclopædia Britannica*. In comparison, the *Britannica* online has about 80,000 entries. If size matters, and it does, there is no way that a curated encyclopedia with articles written by experts and edited by professionals could compete with a product developed by thousands of volunteers writing, editing, correcting, referencing, and linking to outside sources every day, covering every possible subject without any consideration to its possible use or value with no specific audience in mind. In theory, the *Wikipedia* could grow to cover as many topics as humans can imagine. The content of the Wikipedia is basically indistinguishable from the Internet.

Search engines favor several metrics: Large amounts of original content; inbound links; visits to a site; and free and open access without advertising. Because *Wikipedia* has these features, in a search on almost any subject, a *Wikipedia* entry will come up at the top. This makes it almost impossible for any other website that offers the same type of general-information content that has advertising, or has a fraction of its content, or sits behind a paywall, to get as much traffic. Because of its unique attributes, *Wikipedia* became the most popular encyclopedia as well as one of the most visited websites on the Internet. The traditional encyclopedia companies were built around editorial and business models—curated content with fiduciary objectives—that *Wikipedia* intentionally eschewed, and proved that size matters over a smaller, highly curated product, even if the contributors are unknown, the editorial standards undisciplined, and the writing inconsistent.

Only a product born during the digital era could unseat a product like the *Britannica* from its position on top of the encyclopedic food chain, a product that was 250 years in the making but was now handicapped by being in print for most of that time. The *Britannica* may have been the right product for the right time, but it was the wrong product for a time that the founders could never have imagined. Still, the founders had something right: An encyclopedia needed to be comprehensive, relevant, and up to date, which has one meaning when your only option for presenting your content is a printing press and something entirely different in the age of the Internet.

* * *

The publishing and distribution of encyclopedias, multivolume references, phone books, maps, and newspapers, and even CD-ROMs, were based on a one-to-one distribution model, where every unit produced is also sold to an individual or a stand-alone entity, like a library or bookstore, or in the case of CD-ROMs, bundled with a computer. In the chapters that follow, we will see how the publishing environment has changed and how publishers use a variety of formats—print and digital—to personalize content, implement more efficient supply-chains, and utilize digital distribution with a one-to-many model, where one instance of a product lives on a website for an unlimited number of users to access. The development and widespread use of multiple digital formats transforms the way we produce and access information and knowledge.

Notes

1. Telegraph messaging was still in vogue. I often received congratulatory telegrams (birthdays, graduations) from out-of-state relatives and received my first job offer via a Western Union telegram in 1979.

2. According to Statista, in 1960, 78.3% of U.S. housing units had telephones, and by 1970, the percentage shot up to 90%.
3. The first British telephone directory was published in 1880. R.H. Donnelley, the largest U.S. printer at the time, issued a classified, business directory in 1886. According to Donnelley's website, its first cross-reference directory was published in 1917.
4. Some yellow pages are still being printed in some localities. My "North Shore" edition is called "The Real Yellow Pages" and has trademarked the slogan "The original search engine."
5. In 1994, Yahoo! pioneered the first Web directory, called "Jerry [Yang] and David's [Filo] Guide to the World Wide Web." Manually curated and organized into categories (e.g., Sports, Finance, News) by a team of editors, its initial design resembled a print-based directory. By the late 1990s, it had been restructured to compete with other search engines or portals like Lycos and Excite, precursors to Bing and Google.
6. Forty years after the launch of volumes "A" and "B," the 1928 edition of the *OED* finally included all 26 letters in 10 volumes. Continuing to expand over the years, the *OED*'s largest print edition was published in 1989, consisting of 20 volumes.
7. Detail on this can be found in *Public Roads*. "Federal Aid Road Act of 1916: Building the Foundation," by Richard F. Weingroff.
8. Too many times I had the bad luck of looking for a place that was hiding in one of the many creases created by the folds.
9. Unlike the *OED* example discussed earlier, the monthly release schedule for encyclopedias distributed this way was not due to the intense scholarship required to compile and edit each volume, but rather the constraints of the distribution channel; grocery stores did not have the shelf space for hundreds of full sets of encyclopedias.
10. Time-Life's marketing strategy for the various series is discussed in an article by Denny Hatch, "The Rise and Fall of Time-Life Books" in *Target Marketing*, which can be read at The freelibrary.com.
11. This line appeared on the title page of first edition of the "Encyclopaedia Britannica; or, a Dictionary of Arts and Sciences, Compiled upon a New Plan."
12. This slogan appeared on the spines of the eight-volume first edition of the *World Book*.
13. This ratio data is from FundingUniverse.com.

14. The *Britannica* has been adapted and translated into several modern languages, but most European countries, as well as Japan, China, Korea, and Russia in particular, published their own multivolume encyclopedia of similar scope. Although popular for many decades in their respective countries, most of these encyclopedias are no longer in print.
15. In 1990 Britannica, Inc., sold approximately 120,000 sets (or 3.8 million individual volumes) of its flagship the *Britannica* in the U.S alone, and ended print production 20 years later. As of this writing, *World Book* is still available in print. All other multivolume English-language encyclopedias, like the *Encyclopedia Americana*, *Compton's*, and *The New Book of Knowledge*, are no longer in print.
16. World Book claimed to have the world's largest educational direct sales force, with more than 60,000 representatives, many of them full-time teachers working part-time during the summer. Britannica had a smaller sales force, about one-third the size, but they were mostly full-time and called on homes by appointment only. Representatives also exhibited at shopping malls, fairs, trade shows, and rail terminals. Data found in FundingUniverse.com.
17. The cost of the most recent edition of the *Britannica* was approximately $1,400; World Book can be purchased today for $1,100. In 1960, the *World Book* cost $150, or the equivalent of $1,800 after inflation; the *Britannica* cost about $400 in 1960, or $3,500 in today's dollars. One could buy a VW Beetle sedan in 1960 for $1,565. The convertible model would cost about $500 more, or as was sometimes advertised, about $1.00 per pound.
18. The *Britannica*'s first annual supplement, the "Book of the Year," was published in 1938. World Book, Inc., published its first "Year Book" supplement in 1962.
19. The drop-out rate was consistently around 10% per year, but at a slightly larger percentage with customers who had encyclopedias that were more than seven years old.
20. Sales of the *Britannica* dropped precipitously each year between 1992, when the company sold approximately 100,000 sets, and 2012, when the last 8,000 sets still in stock from the final print run in 2010 were sold.
21. On its website World Book describes the image on the Millennium Edition as a sunrise, which is how we described it to the sales force and customers at launch. However, in fact, the image that we licensed from

the photo agency was of a sunset. Fortunately, unless you knew the time of day when the photo was taken, it is hard to tell the difference.
22. Around 1980, Bill Gates, Microsoft's Founder, made this the software company's corporate mission.
23. Microsoft launched *Encarta* in 1993, the online version in 2000, and took down the website in 2009.

1

THE 21ST-CENTURY PUBLISHER

Bridging millennial formats

> Books have the same enemies as people: fire, humidity, animals, weather, and their own content.
>
> —Paul Valery

Print is dead, long live print

In an interview in the procurement and supply-chain newsletter *Spend Matters*, Simon Crump, a printing expert in publishing,[1] discusses the ways in which the processes in every step of the publishing supply chain have been transformed with the introduction of digital printing and the increasing dependence on print-on-demand (POD), or just in time (JIT), and short-run printing. The interview gives a general view of the role that artificial intelligence (AI) and automation in pre-press, data entry, and metadata tagging plays in making it possible for a book to exit a digital printer and be shipped to its destination without being touched by a human being, resulting in cost savings, less waste and loss, and faster time to market.[2] Simon says: "In reality, no one should need to touch your book, from the

DOI: 10.4324/9781003162636-2

moment it is ordered to being printed to being packaged and landing on your doorstep 48 hours later." He implies that the robust investment in AI and automation will continue to improve the efficiency of the publishing value chain, suggesting that a large wager is being made on the future of print. Simon concludes the interview with this comment: "I'm happy to say that people still want the book—there's something comforting about the physical book, especially now at the end of a day of online meetings and studying."[3]

As enthusiastic as Simon is about the benefits of the printed book and what he implies its future may be—backed by ongoing investments in the supply chain—he may be too restrained. Until there is a technology solution that duplicates or improves on the experience we receive from a printed book—the overall look and feel; the variety of readable, typographic styles; the pleasant contrast of ink on paper—and the relatively low cost, books are here to stay.

Everyone loves books in print. Every generation—all around the world, regardless of language and culture—loves books. The physical book is a valued object, not just for the content it holds, but how well it holds it. I would not want two- and three-year-olds to miss the opportunity to grasp a board book in their tiny hands, touch the illustrations, and turn the sturdy pages, back and forth, over and over again, or miss out on the pleasure of discovering the miniature worlds that are revealed in pop-up books, which showcase remarkable paper engineering that makes the three-dimensional displays come to life every time a child turns a page.[4] Personally, I love my collection of "Canterbury Classics"—including the *Complete Works of Shakespeare*, *Charles Dickens* (four novels), a *Mark Twain* anthology of five novels, *The Adventures of Sherlock Holmes*, and seven novels by *Robert Louis Stevenson* bound in one edition—with their genuine leather bindings; embossed, illustrated covers; satin ribbon bookmark; beautifully designed end papers, front and back; ivory-tinted paper; gilded edges (on all three exposed sides); raised, decorative bands (hubs) on the spines; colored headband and tailband on the top and bottom of the book block; and priced between $18 and $22 each depending on page count. It is a pleasure to read books in this format, share them with family members, give them as gifts, and pass them on to the next generation. My wife, on the other hand, cherishes her collection of plain, utilitarian Penguin classic paperbacks. Print has proven to be an excellent medium for the subject matter of these books and most other single titles, especially in attractive binding styles that appeal to a wide variety of individual tastes.

The same way that book lovers feel about physical books, music lovers feel about vinyl records. Most music lovers by this time in the 21st century are consumers of streaming music, which provides an almost unlimited amount of the music you would want to listen to for a monthly fee that is less than the cost of a single vinyl album. Still, some people prefer the way vinyl records sound. Also, with vinyl, you can own the music you really love and enjoy the aesthetics of the album covers and the notes in the inserts about the musicians and performance. Online streaming, while reducing MP3 downloads to irrelevancy, and compact discs (CDs) to near irrelevancy, did not make vinyl obsolete; it just moved it to a different place in the value system.

As I discussed in the Introduction of this book, some categories of books and other reading materials were originally in print only because no other option existed, and today are best suited for use online. The market demand for some types of content in a print version has declined to a degree that it would be fiscally irresponsible for publishers to continue to produce them. Telephone directories should no longer be in print and are mostly extinct. Thick catalogues of office equipment or hardware supplies, not much more than lists of items with little aesthetic appeal, are much easier to use, and would have more current stock information, on a website. Dictionaries are fast and convenient online resources. Multivolume encyclopedias, as discussed earlier, are too costly to produce at the quantities in current demand and are much more sensible in digital form.

For many years, I regularly bought the annual *World Almanac*. Each year's publication replaced the one I had from the year before. I never did love those books, but I found them useful in looking up a quick fact or for ending an argument on the question of the moment, like which movie won the academy award in the best picture category in 1985, or the population of China. Today, the quickest way to get the answer to these kinds of questions is to enter a search on an Internet browser and select one of several reliable sources. For a while, I thought that magazines, whose covers and layouts in print are often extremely attractive, might be worth continuing to receive in print. But the content is perishable, they are not as collectible as books, and the digital versions are much more convenient to use, read, and access on a personal digital device, which also does justice to the design of the original print version.

I do not think there was ever a time when any of us genuinely loved the printed newspaper, with the ink that rubbed off on our hands, the noise it made when we unfolded and re-folded the paper on the commuter train, the air space it took up when we opened it up to its full extent to browse the daily contents. Looking for a particular article was awkward unless it was on the front or last page of the paper. I live in Chicago and the winters are brutal, cold, icy, and for approximately five months, usually starting in early December, we carefully navigate slippery sidewalks and salty streets. One wintery Sunday morning, a couple of years ago, I was walking with my black Labrador Retriever and saw a man in a bathrobe and slippers proceeding cautiously down his driveway to fetch his newspaper. When he finally got to the end of it and bent over to pick up the frozen paper partially covered in snow, he fell on his backside, got up onto his knees, grabbed the paper, and slowly, unsteadily walked back up the driveway. I thought to myself: A video of this scene would make a great public service announcement for going digital.

As soon as e-books hit the market in the early 1990s, the debate began over which format was better, print or e-book, and whether e-books would replace print. Critics made lists of the pros and cons in favor of one over the other. In my book *Dealing with Disruption: Lessons from the Publishing Industry*, I offered my own arguments as well, which are commonplace today. There are advantages and disadvantages to both formats, and each has its own specific attributes and value. One thing is not debatable; unlike eight-track tapes, compact cassettes, or compact discs, print remains an enduring format and was not destined to be a transitional technology as some critics had predicted.

A certain amount of excitement over the advantages of e-books helped to drive the debate as well as the rising fixed costs in producing and delivering printed books. E-books were cheaper to produce, easier to distribute, and could hit the market much quicker. As is the case with most technology solutions, the cost of producing e-books was likely to go down as well. Today, the "one-to-many" distribution model for e-books, which only requires the publisher to launch a single instance of it on a website and have it retrieved by an unlimited number of users, is much cheaper and faster than the "one-to-one" model for print. Publishers were worried about the future cost of paper and ink and the labor involved in a printed product, as well as cost of shipping books from overseas printers and risking losing the product in the ocean. E-books do not carry these risks.

Print has an illustrious past, but its future was being questioned in the face of digital content. The backdrop, of course, was how quickly music formats transitioned from the earliest formats, vinyl records (until they made a comeback in a niche market) and reel-to-reel recording tape, to eight-track cassettes, compact cassettes, compact discs (CDs), MP3 downloads, and finally on-demand streaming services.[5]

The perception of being stuck in the past was on the minds of consumers and publishers. In the mid-1990s, some publishers worried about appearing as Luddites and started to bundle a CD-ROM with a printed book for the same price as the book alone so a consumer would not have to choose one format over the other and enjoy the added benefits of the new media on the disc. I am holding a book in my hands right now called *Digital Business*, published in 1996, that includes a CD-ROM with an online edition of the book and Netscape Navigator, which I assume was required to view the digital version. Given the nature of the 286-page book, the CD-ROM does not include any media or add any value to the reading experience; it is more of a marketing tool than a useful add-on. Plus, 25 years after the book was published, I can still read it, but the CD-ROM is incompatible with current technology, and has been for at least ten years.

The publishing of printed books, separate from any relationship with technology supplements, remains a viable business if it is managed well and used for the appropriate content. And the right books do not need any help from additional media. It is moot to argue the superiority or inferiority of digital outputs over print, or whether print will ever be replaced if it remains profitable for all participants in the supply chain. Television did not replace radio (though broadcast was largely replaced by cable, which in turn may eventually be replaced by the Internet). Podcasts, which are meant to be more evergreen in nature, will probably not replace live radio, which broadcasts perishable content meant for everyday consumption. But small technology advances can have a large impact on consumer preferences as well as costs, so publishers need to stay abreast of consumer sentiment and what market forces tell us about consumer trends rather than fads; keep track of what consumers' reading behavior reveals about format positioning—when to use print or the most efficient technology; and adjust their business models to stay competitive and profitable.

Print and digital formats separately and together increase the publishers' options for providing consumers with enhanced reading and learning experiences, either bundled together or linked in some way. However, access to Internet products is still a problem for a good portion of the global population. Publishers and content developers cannot assume that they will be able to reach 100% of the market with digital products, though they can make that assumption about print. And for many products, publishers should not abandon a meaningful percentage of the market by dropping print if it remains profitable.

Even as we have seen the costs of digital products go down over time, print will continue to move in the opposite direction, though we do not know how fast. The laptop I am working on now, with 16GB of RAM and a terabyte of storage, along with a superfast processor and HD screen, was about one-third the cost of the first Apple Macintosh computer that I bought for my daughter 25 years ago, and that computer, with its tiny screen, had about as much computing capability as today's calculators, or maybe less. At the same time, printed books have gone up in price at the pace of inflation. Even so, I will argue that books in print are a bargain.

Still, there are three business concerns that print publishers cannot overlook, even though they have not proved to be fatal: The cost of paper, minimum print quantities required for traditional printing presses, and time to market. As a fixed cost, paper represents approximately 30% of the total cost of a print product, and only rises over time. Increasing costs of paper must either be passed on to the consumer or taken from publishers' margins. Thus, publishers, working with printers and paper mills (or brokers), need to optimize the entire supply chain to ensure that the total cost of printing and shipping does not escalate. Fortunately, technology—advances in digital printing in particular—has provided some solutions that can keep these costs under check so as not to create a dramatic price rise for the end-user or eat into publishers' margins.

Before digital printers, printing large quantities of a title on offset printers was the only way that publishers could mitigate unit costs. Due to the fixed makeready costs inherent in traditional printing, the higher the quantity of units produced, the lower the per-unit costs. High-volume printing is handled by either sheet-fed offset or web offset printers. Web offset printers are used for exceptionally long runs, newspapers, for example, or multivolume print products. Both sheet-fed offset and web offset printers, given the long print runs, are more economical per unit than digital printing, but they burden the publisher with managing inventory and storage costs. If publishers are confident that they will sell all that they print, or they have pre-publication orders that cover the print run, they should use offset printing to keep their unit costs as low as possible—the more they print the lower the cost. In general, for print runs of at least 1,000 units, offset printing produces the lowest costs per unit.

Short-run printing (SRP) or printing-on-demand (POD) are digital technology-driven solutions that do not require the higher, minimum quantities of long-run printing. With POD, publishers will pay more per each unit produced than they would by committing to a long print run, but with POD or SRP, they do not have to commit to a minimum number of units that they may eventually have to either remainder at prices below their cost or destroy. Print-on-demand is a great solution for books that sell slowly. Through online distributors, like Amazon, a customer can order a single copy of a book, which can be printed "on demand," with no existing inventory in stock. Print-on-demand is also a good solution for self-publishers who do not want any inventory exposure and need only a small quantity at any time. The quality of POD is quite good, particularly for black and white books, though quality does diminish slightly for four-color books. Short-run printing requires the publisher to commit to a minimum of 100 units, but the quality is better than from typical POD outputs and the per-unit price is lower.

Having these digital printing solutions available has enabled small, specialty publishers to print titles that they thought they could only afford to publish as e-books and has enabled large publishers to keep in print slow-selling titles, or titles that have peaked in sales that they thought would eventually go out of print. Thanks to SRP and POD, books no longer need to go out of print. Titles that would have reached their end of life, perhaps after the stock had been remaindered or even destroyed, can have an extended life with POD. Short-run printing and POD have been lifeboats for small- to medium-sized publishing companies, affording them the ability to publish books that are far from being best-sellers but are in demand for a small niche audience.

Catherine Bruzzone, the Founder of b small publishing, a children's language publisher in the United Kingdom, uses SRP to supply her customers with print products at a reasonable price, and fulfill orders almost instantly. Because the number of copies she sells of any given title is small, she is not interested in making an investment in a large print run that would drive unit costs down as low as possible from a traditional offset printer. Instead, by using SRP, she can order fewer copies from a digital printer and go back for additional quantities as needed. Even though she pays a slightly higher price per unit than she would if she ran the title on an offset press, she has a much lower upfront cost, does not worry about having excess inventory, and can meet her customers' demand.

Catherine's goal is to maximize total cost of ownership (TCO) rather than achieve the lowest unit cost. If she invested in a long print run using an offset press, she would lower her immediate per unit costs, but over time, a long print run might cost her more. Not only would she have the capital expense in the inventory, but she would also have warehousing charges and may have excess inventory if sales do not go as expected, thus, in the end, raising her per-unit costs. With SRP, she accomplishes two objectives for the benefit of her bottom line—she avoids having to make a large cash outlay in inventory, and she does not have to tell customers that a title is on back order. She describes the benefits of SRP in this way:

We publish in a niche market, but we knew that our "Let's Read" bilingual stories for children were appreciated by the teachers and bilingual families that tried them; but we just could not afford to do standard reprints to keep them on sale. After trying several suppliers, we realized that the set-up costs meant POD [print-on-demand] would not work for book retailing at only £6.99 [$9.60]. They are also full-color books and with very thin spines. We found the solution was short-run printing from Ashford Press: Printing 100 copies at a time, just enough stock to keep them ticking along and financially viable.

For Catherine, and many publishers in the same marketing situation with a list of narrowly targeted publications—almost any title that is not a "best-seller"—SRP is a viable alternative to offset printing, which would have lowered her unit costs but would have increased her inventory commitment from 100 to 1,000 units and kept her customers waiting for delivery for five to six weeks.

Short-run printing and offset printing are options for publishers depending on their position in the market and how much inventory they believe they can move. (Increasingly, these kinds of decisions are data driven, but some guesswork cannot be avoided.) At the same time, POD provides a way for the publisher to relinquish control of ordering print products to the hands of the customer. By making their products available through online distributor websites, publishers can offer individual customers their products on demand. The publisher does not have to worry about stock levels and the customer does not have to worry about waiting for the publisher to receive a new supply of books.

Victor Rivero, the Editor-in-Chief of EdTech Digest, a periodical that serves the educational publishing industry, used POD to avoid the risk of investing in a large inventory of a new series without knowing how well they would be received. Victor describes the situation this way:

Our publication covers leaders, innovators, and trendsetters in education and technology across the K-12, higher education, and workforce sectors. In addition to content regularly published through our site, we had been contemplating a series of sponsored guides for educators and parents. Discovery Education, Aruba Networks, and others were interested; the question was: Do we take the leap and risk of an expensive print run and distribute them through the mail and at trade shows, of which our industry has many? Or do we simply stick with digital? We ended up producing a PDF document of magazine-quality design that could be printed on demand. We pushed it out as a link—leading to a high-resolution download with an email catcher—to tens of thousands through our subscriber list, and for those wanting to print it, they could print individual copies on demand at an Office Depot, at their company office, or given current times (meaning the Covid-19 pandemic), their home office. Or they could simply view it on their devices. Advertisers came back for more, and readers did as well. A combination of rich content and easy-on-the-eyes design were a large part of the success that this turned out to be.

Solving the print dilemma digitally

Publishers of disparate publications—professional journals, academic or professional monographs, specialty publications, for example—all can take advantage of the technology that makes low-quantity print runs possible. The vendors who work with publishers and guide them through the best way to solve their printing challenges are now addressing several business issues at the same time. The most successful partners enable publishers to play to their strengths of producing quality books with relevant, highly targeted content—the typical core competencies of a professional publisher—and provide services throughout the entire supply chain that help publishers maximize their margins, starting with advice on the paper, binding, and the most efficient printing method based on the goals of the project, and concluding with putting products in the hands of readers. In between these goalposts, their project plan should reduce or eliminate inventory costs, avoid obsolescence, and even partially finance product placement with distributors, retailers, and libraries. Publisher expenses are thus reduced, lowering, or eliminating distribution costs, leaving them only with costs associated with their core competency—editorial resources, royalty payments, and sales and marketing expenses.

The publishing industry in India has made tremendous advances in providing logistic and printing solutions for publishers both inside and outside India. Pre-press and printing companies have positioned themselves as valuable outsource providers for more than 25 years, in part due to their level of education and training, large literate population in English as a first language, technology expertise, and lower wage levels.

Repro India, one of India's largest book producers and exporters, pioneered what Director Dushyant Mehta describes as a "technology-based content aggregation solution." Working directly with online distributors (like Amazon and Walmart) offering print-on-demand books directly to the end-user, Repro provides a turnkey solution and liberates publishers from much of the post-production costs in getting books to the market. Dushyant describes the process this way:

> It begins when the publisher submits printer-ready PDFs (portable document format) to us and we hold the files in our digital repository and list them, with specified metadata (meaning keywords that uniquely identify the file), for online distributors of books, like Amazon, or library and school distributors. We also provide a website portal for B2B sales to distributors, retailers, schools, and libraries and work with the publisher to help generate demand through these channels. When books are ordered by the end-consumer, we print the book using our on-demand digital printers.

The finished product can be produced in black and white or color, in a variety of trim sizes, with hard or soft binding. The customer can receive the books as quickly as 24 hours, depending on shipping methods and destination. The publisher receives their royalty directly from us and pays any outstanding author royalties from these funds. In this scenario, the publisher has no upfront investment in print inventory and warehousing, with the additional benefits of no returns, obsolescence, or logistics costs. Most of the publisher's working capital can be devoted to producing the book and almost zero to the supply chain.

With this kind of printing solution, the publisher can plan for a quicker and better return on their investment for each title and a lower capital outlay. In constructing an ROI on any single title, the publisher starts with the amount of capital necessary to develop the book, including any author advances. With digital publishing, the publisher does not have to set aside funds for post-production functions, significantly increasing their margins as well. Publishers also eliminate any losses due to bad debt since payments are due to the printer at the time of ordering. In addition, since the catalogue of titles is available online, distribution can now be global, and products can be purchased in local currency. Investments in marketing, promoting, and building awareness are not fixed costs, so these efforts can be dialed up or down at the publisher's discretion. These costs exist regardless of how books are produced—it is neither an additional cost nor a cost savings with a digital printing solution.

Two other advantages of this turnkey solution are worth mentioning: Time to market, which is significantly quicker with digital printing so a publisher can shorten the time it takes to get a return on investment; and market adaptability—by using a technology platform, the publisher can ramp up scale or change direction depending on market demand.

* * *

Unlike e-books, which exist in cyberspace, printed books are part of the physical world and have unique costs associated with any product that needs to be manufactured and shipped one unit at a time. With digital books, publishers can produce one "virtual instance," upload it on a server, and have an unrestricted number of people grab a digital copy and download it—one-to-many publishing. Users should realize that they do not really own their "copy" of the digital publication; it is a license to use the file, even if that license is in perpetuity. We can think about this just like a photographer licenses his or her photo for use in a publication. The photographer retains the original photo, which can be the basis for an infinite number of uses, or licenses. For publishers, the publishing of digital books is a way of getting around the one-to-one costs of printed books, and why savings throughout the supply chain will always be a management priority.

The consumer may see the differences between digital and printed books differently, because e-books may be cheaper to purchase, but they require an electronic device, are personal, and cannot be used on someone else's device. And there is always the concern that at some point the software that runs the device will be incompatible with the digital book, which at some point may be unable to be read. Printed books, on the other hand, provide long-term value, are always accessible, and do not require any outside help.

Our local library, which was established in 1887 and made its first book purchases in 1888, still has some books in its collection that date back to its founding. Thousands of books in the library's collection are decades old, and almost all of them continue to be in circulation and are as readable as when they were first published. My son, who was home from college during the pandemic, checked out a copy of Dostoyevsky's *Demons*, in a 1998 English translation of the Russian novel written in 1871. The 23-year-old translation looked like it had not been read, even though it had been checked out many times. The library also has a section dedicated to media, movies, and music, which, in the past, received more interest from patrons than the book stacks. While the print books have retained their value and use over many decades, the media section has gone through an entire collection of movies in VHS, which the library then had to replace with DVDs. Now obsolete, those discs too became obsolete and were recently either sold off, given away, or destroyed. Meanwhile the library's investment in printed books has continued to grow in importance and value, if for no other reason than patrons are still able to check out and use any of the books in the collection regardless of when they were published.

Personally, we have had three children read the same copies of *The Tale of Peter Rabbit*, *Goodnight Moon*, the Berenstain Bears series, *Winnie the Pooh*, *Madeleine*, and dozens of other classic children's books written and published from the 1930s through the 1980s that we purchased a little more than 30 years ago when my oldest daughter was a toddler. Over the last few months, we have been boxing up these gems and sending them to my daughter's home in Los Angeles, where our three-year-old grandson can enjoy them. Now he can read the same books with his mother that she read with hers. But because a publisher sells their books only once to an individual, a library, or through a bookstore, the long-lasting value of the books that they had printed and sold years in the past has no bearing on their current ROI considerations when they publish the next *Crime and Punishment*, *Beloved*, or *The Fault in Our Stars*.

Notes

1. The interview, titled "Procurement in Practice," is in the January 11, 2021, issue, © Azul Partners.
2. The big breakthrough in digital printing came in 1991. Unlike offset printing, which uses replaceable printing plates, digital printing methodology prints directly on paper (or some other medium), from a digitally produced image. Also, digital printing can be done locally, close to the destination, radically improving time to market.
3. When he says, "especially now," he is referring to the ongoing Covid-19 pandemic.
4. Different types of pop-up books, sometimes referred to as movable books, can include flaps, pull tabs (up or down), pop-outs, tunnels (for looking through a series of scenes), volvelles (rotating parts, like a wheel chart), and pocket inserts.
5. Compact cassettes were invented in 1963, a year or so before eight-track tapes, but only gained popularity in the late 1970s after eight-tracks had peaked and started to decline. Compact discs were released to the public shortly thereafter, in 1982. MP3 files for downloading music arrived in 1993, but the first successful download service came in 2003 with Apple's iTunes store. Launched in 2005, Pandora is considered the first music streaming service.

2

PRINT AND DIGITAL HYBRIDS

First inklings

> I don't need to know everything, I just need to know where to find it, when I need it.
>
> —**Albert Einstein**

I was reading Steven Pinker's *Enlightenment Now: The Case for Reason, Science, Humanism, and Progress* (2018), and halfway through the 540-page, data-rich tome, I tried to recall a list that I read earlier in the book of false beliefs that were commonly held by an educated English populace during the first-half of the 17th century.[1] One of those false beliefs, among many kooky ones—like witches can summon up storms that sink ships at sea; mice are spontaneously generated in piles of straw; it's possible to turn base metal into gold, but no one knows how; dreams predict the future—was "nature abhors a vacuum."[2] I did not remember where in the book I read this, and it was not referenced in the index. I shuffled through the pages trying to find it with no luck. Like looking for a needle in a haystack.

I got out my iPad and opened my local library app, found the e-book version of *Enlightenment Now*, downloaded it, typed "false beliefs" in the search box, and . . . eureka, found it instantly on page nine. I am willing to accept that this may not be a typical use case for e-books since I did not want to read the entire book in this format but rather needed to pinpoint a specific phrase, and it was the only time that I used it; nor would it be a persuasive reason for a publisher to include a link in the hardback book to an e-book app just to address the occasional need of a compulsive reader like me. More likely a regular e-book user will value the convenience of an e-book, separate from a printed book, for its portability and functionality on an electronic device like a Kindle, tablet, iPhone, or laptop. Nonetheless, the e-book was right tool at the right time for me. I "returned" the e-book after I found what I was looking for and continued to read the rest of Pinker's book—which I highly recommend—in print.

If there were a singular product that would enable the reader to slip easily and seamlessly between print and digital experiences, and priced like a typical hardback book, I would think that it would be well received. It would allow the reader who prefers a printed book to take advantage of the handy functionality of many e-books—like searching for a word or phrase; bookmarking multiple pages; accessing an embedded dictionary; tapping/clicking a chapter head in the table of contents to go immediately to the right page; changing the color of the text page (sepia, black, or white out of black); adjusting the font size; tapping/clicking left or right to go page by page, or scrolling a slider rule to find any page quickly; tracking how much time spent reading the book; highlighting in one of several colors; and copying text—without having to acquire each format separately. The e-book does have its advantages as a standalone product, though, even if the user experience of the printed book for many readers trumps the digital-only features.

According to Ian Grant, the co-Founder of the London-based production company Creative Structure, despite the need for technology-driven products, "there is a demand for new print editions of major classic works, even scholarly multivolume texts, from research libraries, academic institutions, practitioners in academic and professional disciplines, and in some cases even a broader readership." Ian believes that the publisher's focus must be on the reader's experience with both the print and digital products. He puts it this way:

The challenge to publishers, which includes the economics of creating, printing, and distributing major printed editions, is how

to balance the reader's experience of close examination of a printed text with the editorial, typographic, design, and coding requirements of a digital edition of the same material.

In a current publication of a specific work, the emerging answer is to lay down the foundations of the editorial matter in the electronic edition. In this set of files, the original text, the revisions and updates, editorial corrections, emendations, and new additions are collated and identified. Clicking on a highlighted word or passage reveals the history of changes from a previous edition. This mass of information would be daunting to a reader of a printed edition. In print, the editorial apparatus is stripped back to a level at which the reader's experience is comfortable and unhindered. The reader's attention is drawn, sensitively, visually, to major emendations, corrections, and updating. In today's publishing, we must assume that readers of the printed edition who want to research further in the huge electronic reservoir of detailed editorial material will have or acquire access to it.

By emphasizing the role that a digital version can play in making aspects of the work beyond reading available to a reader who wants background information and to see the "scaffolding" behind the words that they are reading, both the digital and print formats have complementary purposes, and one strengthens the other in providing data to the reader. With care and great expertise from today's editors, typographers, designers, digital architects, printers, and binders, even the largest multivolume works can be published in enlightening, attractive complementary formats.

The idea of bundling or linking print with technology applications is not a new one. Product concepts that physically combined an e-book on a CD-ROM with the printed book started to appear in the market in a variety of publishing categories, especially with children's books, in the mid-1990s. Some CD-ROMs provided sound effects and additional visuals to supplement the books, but they mostly seemed like marketing strategies rather than a product extension that a reader would frequently use—something akin to a toy in a cereal box. The first time I encountered a successful example of combining print and CD-ROM technology that enhanced the user's experience with the content of the book was with dictionaries, a technology feature now commonly embedded in most e-book formats and productivity software like Microsoft Word. In 1995, Merriam-Webster, the premier U.S. dictionary publisher, marketed its flagship hardback, thumb-indexed *Collegiate Dictionary* together with a CD-ROM that contained the entire contents of the dictionary with search capabilities and pronunciations—the latter being a welcomed feature over the arcane pronunciation codes used in all print dictionaries. John Morse, the president and publisher of Merriam-Webster at the time, thought that with the advent of the CD-ROM, "we entered the 'age of also,' and we published the print dictionary with a CD-ROM version for the same price as the hardback edition," setting the stage for technology and print bundles that would be a useful publishing solution for a range of reference books. Since a dictionary is normally used only occasionally and not read cover to cover like literature, the CD-ROM was a replacement for the printed book, which had no advantages over the digital version unless you did not have a computer, or your electricity, or Wi-Fi went out.

As a "look-up" tool, a single-volume dictionary has much more in common with a multivolume reference work than it does with most other stand-alone books, and like multivolume references is much better suited for a digital platform than a bound printed book. John envisioned a suite of these "hybrid" print/technology products with his other dictionaries (e.g., medical, legal, crossword puzzle, learner's, Spanish-English), and was convinced that consumers would enthusiastically embrace the "age of also"— a term coined by the information architect Richard Saul Wurman—even when the Internet made the CD-ROM obsolete and accelerated a dramatic reduction in the sales of print dictionaries. John described his team's strategy at the time this way:

We looked upon the Web, or the dictionary in digital form, as in effect an endorsement of the dictionary's quality, and hence actually supportive of print. In other words, if you like us on the Web, you'll be more inclined to buy us in print. The phrase "age of also" hadn't been coined yet, but I think we were guided by that concept, nonetheless.[3]

Even though print/technology bundles for dictionaries did not last long as a viable consumer product once the Web versions became the most convenient and reliable source for looking up words for their spelling, definition, and pronunciation, John was on the right track with the potential value of combining different formats to enhance the consumer experience. The "age of also" captures only the initial period of blending digital and analog formats to leverage the best of both outputs. Here's Wurman's turn-of-the-century vision of how "also" could improve consumers' access to information and knowledge (prior to the demise of the DVD and before the dominance of the Web) in the future:

Well, certainly, the next 10–15 years will be the age of "also." I mean, we're going to have print, we're going to have books. We're going to have better magazines and more magazines, better newspapers, and different newspapers. We're going to have TV and we're going to have satellite. We're going to have computers. We are going to have computers that are TV. We're going to have DVD. We're going to have lots of things. Will there be some falling outs? You bet. We don't have eight-track sound anymore, and in the future, tapes will eventually die out because everybody will have CDs, and then CDs will die out because there'll just be one thing, which will be DVD for both images and sound. But for the next 10–15 years, we'll also have a bunch of things going on, all at the same time. And that's fine. There isn't a best answer for things, anymore. There's not a best way to have transportation. There's not a best way of communicating. There's not a best way for anything. There are just good ways.[4]

Many combinations of books and CD-ROMs that complemented each other successfully—where the CD-ROM added sound, images, and interactivities to the book's basic text—came out in the mid-1990s. At World Book, I forged a partnership with a U.K. company called Two-Can that was known for the "fun-fact" inserts they created for the weekend edition of the *Young Telegraph*. An innovative children's publisher, Two-Can started early in the rush to add technology to print by first including floppy discs to the *Young Telegraph* newspaper content. They also had a creative children's book publishing department that specialized in highly illustrated nonfiction books for libraries and classrooms. Together we created a series of books-plus-CD-ROMs that we called "Interfact," which paired a 48-page wire-o-bound book with a CD-ROM on nature and history topics like *Deserts*, *Caves*, and

Volcanoes; *Seals, Elephants, and Tigers*; and *Ancient Greece, Ancient Rome, and The Aztecs*. We sold each book and CD-ROM bundle in a neat, custom-designed case for £9.99 ($13.70). (Recently I discovered a copy of *Volcanoes* on e-Bay.) We regarded the first two pages of the book as the most "innovative" part of the product since they explained succinctly what exactly was on the disc, whose contents in similar hybrid products on the market were usually a mystery until the user deployed the CD-ROM. Our objective was to include the kind of content in the books that worked best on the printed page (clear text, relevant images, infographics) while dedicating the CD-ROMs to games, puzzles, interactivities, and animations not possible to render in print—to blend the two formats so that the users feel that they are getting a great value, that in this case, one plus one equals three.

If we were to do these titles today, the media complements would most likely include videos, recorded speech (as opposed to machine generated text-to-speech), and virtual reality (VR) accessed via an app on a tablet or computer. A book about the stars and planets, for example, could make use of VR to display three-dimensional renderings of constellations. Artificial Intelligence (AI) could be used to keep track of vocabulary that the reader looks up while reading passages or factoids on the disc for generating a review quiz. Some innovative children's products on the market today do all of this and more.

As early examples of using the best features from print and digital formats to engage the reader in ways that each format cannot do alone, the "Interfact" titles were extremely popular. Ian Grant, of Creative Structures, who also happened to be one of the founders of Two-Can, reminded me recently of a trip he and his son made to the Arctic in the late 1990s where they discovered a copy of the Interfact title *Polar Lands* in a bookshop there. Obviously, the work of a very intuitive, proactive North American sales rep. However, you would think that the Arctic market had enough real-life knowledge of the frozen tundra and that the bookshop might attract more customer interest in, say, *Deserts* or *Tropical Rainforests*.

Conversion pains

Today, publishers release their new front list titles in both print and e-book formats, and increasingly as audiobooks. If a book is issued in a hardback edition, it might be released ahead of the e-book and the paperback versions, but not always. The two print, e-book, and audiobook formats are all independent entities and are sold separately. Since the CD-ROM with e-book combinations are a product of a different time, the multiple formats that books are typically available in is not strictly an extension of the "age of also" as Wurman envisioned it, but they each have their own market and are in demand, with upward trending sales. While there continues to be a strong market for books in both print and e-book formats, traditional publishers—meaning professional publishing houses as opposed to the growing number of self-publishers—sell far more books in print than e-books, and earn more top-line revenue from print, which not only accounts for more unit sales but also a higher percentage of revenue. Depending on the year and the data source, of any given title, approximately 80% of sales will come from print and 20% e-books.[5] In any case, print is still king.

The e-book-to-print comparison is somewhat like comparing apples to oranges. While the markets for the two formats overlap, the e-book market is smaller in part because of its dependency on technology. Barriers to a potentially higher penetration of e-book sales include the cost of the e-reader or electronic device needed for e-book downloads; the personal nature of e-books, i.e., they are dedicated to one individual and cannot be shared or resold; and the lack of a second-hand market. For self-publishers, e-books most likely account for a larger percentage of their book sales than print, but it's hard to say exactly since Amazon, which accounts for most of the self-publishing sales in the United States and United Kingdom, does not share its statistics.

When traditional publishers convert their print-based products into e-books, or when they go straight from final layouts to a digital output, they have to choose from several different e-book formats, and typically produce their e-books in three different formats: Epub, or PDF for customers to download directly from the publishers' sites and for most third-party distributors, and mobi or azw, proprietary Amazon formats for their Kindle and Fire devices. Except for Amazon, epub has become a de facto standard. Still, even within epub and mobi, publishers need to choose between fixed and reflowable layouts—whether the text should flow, like a text-heavy book when the user changes the size of the font or with different screen sizes; or remain "fixed," like a highly illustrated book, where the integrity of the design needs to remain intact and the text and images can't move around, or "flow."

Most publishers are producing their titles in both print and e-book formats to maximize their sales and revenue opportunities. The availability of e-books does not seem to have cannibalized print sales but rather has created a new market. Although sales of e-books are much lower than print, publishers can get access to the digital market relatively easily and economically by repurposing the same intellectual property they developed for the print version—basically using the same content in a different format. Publishers can leverage all the editorial they invested in creating a print book for making an e-book with only minor additional technology costs. It may not be two formats for the price of one, exactly, since there are some conversion costs in making a print product digital, but the cost of converting most books is a fraction of the sunk costs of creating the original book. Highly illustrated books with varying layouts throughout the book require more resources to convert than a standard black-and-white book. Still, even these conversions do not add an excessive amount of cost to the production process unless the publisher includes additional media, links to video, for example, or recorded speech. But these decisions should be based on the publisher's assessment of the additional market a book will attract with the added features, or how much more the publisher can charge.

On behalf of their patrons, librarians also expect to buy any book in a publisher's front- or backlist in print as their priority and obtain download licensing privileges to the e-book formats that are available, which is another incentive for publishers to offer both digital and print formats. Although e-books continue to grow in popularity, licensing rights options that libraries obtain from publishers, which they make available to their patrons in the form of usage rights, have not been resolved. For example, revenue sharing with e-book distributors has not been standardized and can vary by as much as 30%–40% depending on the distributor; and publishers are inconsistent in how they charge libraries for e-book licensing rights, which can vary from unlimited downloading privileges to only one download at a time, i.e., a second patron would not be able to download a specific e-book title until the first patron "returns" it. Publishers do not actually sell digital books; they license the rights to use them. And you do not actually own the e-books that you "purchase"; you rent them, either in perpetuity at full price, or for a defined time for a lower price.[6] Even though the content of the e-books is the same as the print books you own, they are marketed more like software. From a publisher's perspective, they have different risk factors (for example, to protect the authors' royalties by ensuring that all downloads are counted, and to prevent piracy) than printed books, which bring a unique set of costs to consider for calculating an acceptable return on investment. Here is one example of how a publisher weighs the risks and rewards of producing e-books.

Catherine Bruzzone, as the Founder of b small publishing, a small children's press, must tightly control her costs, and because of her long experience creating illustrated children's books, has a particularly good idea of how many copies of each book she will sell—so she can forecast revenue—and knows precisely how much she should invest in the development of each book to make a sufficient margin. By the mid-2000s, she was aware that many publishers were finding a fertile market for their existing titles if they converted them to e-books. She learned from publishing colleagues that e-books not only provide a new revenue stream and generate better margins than the print counterparts—and even better margins when you are able to market both—and was surprised to hear that the effort involved in creating the e-book versions was relatively minimal. But she also learned that how you define success depends on managing expectations. E-books will generate incremental revenue at a relatively low cost, but they probably won't change a publisher's fortunes.

We had the dubious advantage of getting quite early into e-books for our bilingual children's stories, *I Can Read* series (for ages 3–8) and *Let's Read* series (for ages 6+). In 2012, when all the talk was e-books, e-books, e-books, a very enthusiastic tech consultant created an easy-to-use template for us. Then we were lucky enough to give (paid) work experience to a student who had just finished a music technology course and had the skills to use the template to create e-books from our print files. While he slogged away at this, we had another lucky break. A new customer in Japan was looking for e-books for the ELT (English language teaching) market, which he was convinced was about to explode. A rights sale to him covered our costs of creating the e-books, and we were able to launch 28 titles for Kindle and Apple Books with no direct costs. I wrote "dubious" advantage above as, despite our early entry into digital books, they did not get us to El Dorado, and we only had a trickle of sales. Print books are still the key products for the children's trade market, and, as a micro-publisher, we don't have the resources to promote more widely and increase our income.

Transition, transition!

Catherine's experience is from the point of view of a traditional children's publisher with a print-centric market and traditional distributors, licensees, and retailers. She is publishing all of her books now in e-book and audiobook formats, which allow her language books to "speak." Over time, and with an increased effort in marketing, her e-book and audiobook sales will increase, even if they remain a fraction of print sales.

With the availability of print and digital options, including websites and apps, publishers can present content to address specific market needs (like foreign-language learners), which is not possible with print alone or older technology. Before the easy access to digital content, to enhance the content of the printed book to make the information either "come alive," or to better illustrate what is presented on the printed page with sound or video, publishers settled for clumsy consumer packages that combined print and technology that not only made for awkward consumer experiences but added production costs that either diluted their margins or was passed on to the consumer.

Jane Wightwick, an Oxford-based Founder, and publisher of the best-selling Arabic-language series *Mastering Arabic*, went through great pains to pair printed books with audiocassettes to deliver learners of Arabic a near-native experience. Being able to replace the audiocassettes, and then the CDs, with a website, made a huge difference in her cost structure and delivered a better consumer experience. But because of the design requirements of her bilingual Arabic-English course book, she was unable to transfer the learning process completely to the screen; she still needed the print material. She describes her transition from analog publishing to the 21st century as "a story of language learning over three decades":

Mastering Arabic was first published in 1990. A typesetter with specialist machinery and operators was needed for the bi-directional English-Arabic "bromide galleys." [With Arabic reading from right to left and English left to right.] All the illustrations and photos were sized and scanned and then the elements were pasted onto boards. These processes required many checking and design stages (and a lot of expense!). But at least we now had cassettes – this was language learning after all. We even managed to record them in a professional studio rather than in a broom cupboard.

Skip to the latest edition in 2020. The single black and white *Mastering Arabic* title is now a successful stable of seven color titles (core courses, activity books, supplementary books). The bi-directional layout is still specialist, but only requires someone skilled in operating the bi-lingual software loadable on any computer. Gone are the cassettes (or CDs for that matter), and now all the audio is available online. This has been joined on the **free** "companion" website by specially recorded videos, flashcards, games, reference sheets, additional activities, and more. In fact, when we have finished revising an element of the program, we joke that the work has only just started.

We need the companion website to give the learner more options and a sense of control, and to keep up with the competition. The balance is to make the core book still necessary—and currently it is since the material is "design critical": No screen can reproduce the flexibility of the printed page in such a niche market. Plus, we need something to bring us publishing income; "you can't eat websites," as my co-author says.

So, we hover between the two worlds of physical and online delivery and it works, for the moment!

The age of also, if we continue to regard the simultaneous publication of various outputs in this way, has allowed the publisher to further delight the reader, make improvements in their delivery because of user input, and create additional publications based on data from consumer engagement with the product. In addition to e-books, audiobooks, and websites, publishers and authors are using blogs and podcasts to continue the conversation that may have been started in print. Subscribers to many monthly magazines can listen to podcasts based on the articles in print, the authors can have a dialog with readers by posting blogs, and the publisher drops additional articles as they are published in between the monthly downloads. By creating a life for a publication beyond its sellable components and engaging with consumers well after they purchased the publication regardless of format, publishers accomplish two things at once: They extend the value of their brand and extend the lifetime value of their customers.

At the end of John Doerr's bestselling book *Measure What Matters*, published in 2018—well into the age of also—he invites the reader to "continue the conversation" by going to his website at whatmatters.com. Although his book contains many behind-the-scenes stories of how companies develop and measure corporate objectives and "key results," the website allows the reader to learn more through a wider variety of examples and a larger pool of relevant models to relate to. But he goes even further by providing his email address, inviting readers to "join the discussion," like I did at the end of the preface in this book. I signed up to receive his team's newsletter at whatmatters.com, which provides additional content on the themes of the book and gives his readers an opportunity to join a *Measure What Matters* community of people committed to improving business metrics and increasing individual productivity. In this way, the publisher and author can engage with consumers past the initial sale of the book and not only contribute to their readers' knowledge and skills, but their lifestyle as well.

Notes

1. Pinker cites historian David Wootton's book *The Invention of Science: A New History of the Scientific Revolution*. (Harper Collins) as his source for the list.
2. This idiom, *horror vacui*, attributed to Aristotle, jumped out at me because, as a 21st century, educated American, I thought it was true. Apparently, it has been debunked; but I do not think it is as clearly batty as the other false beliefs in the list, like "werewolves . . . are to be found in Belgium."
3. Richard Saul Wurman, the founder of the TED conference, used the phrase "age of also" to suggest that different formats, both analog and digital, should be used to create products that enhance the learning experience.
4. *Ubiquity*, Volume 2000 Issue, March 2000, Article No. 1, by John Gehl.
5. Since 2017, audiobooks have represented the fastest-growing category in publishing, but they do not match e-book sales. Increasingly, publishers have been switching to a subscription model for audiobooks, like streaming music services, which might increase their revenue from this format but will inevitably lower sales of individual downloads.

6. In theory, your rights to the e-book you license via a download may be perpetual, but in practice there may be a time in the future when the downloaded file is no longer compatible with the device on which it has been downloaded. This is a risk that the consumer takes. Some publishers will permit the free transference of e-book files from on format to another, but this practice is not consistent and often depends on the e-book distributor.

3

DATA, METADATA, AND HUMANS

> I never guess. It is a capital mistake to theorize before one has data. Insensibly one begins to twist facts to suit theories, instead of theories to suit facts.
> —**Sir Arthur Conan Doyle**, *The Sign of Four, A Scandal in Bohemia*

When publishing was bound by the constraints of an analog world, it was possible to know the total number of new titles, journals, magazines, films, and programs—any kind of published material—that we were producing or consuming daily. Granted, it would have been an extremely large number, but, in theory, it would have been possible to count them all. Today, as we have been producing digital books and other consumer-facing digital content for more than 25 years, we could not begin to calculate all the active publishers, let alone the number of publications viewable or retrievable from various databases.[1]

The world is now brimming with self-publishers and what I would describe as micropublishers, like bloggers or vloggers (video bloggers), growing each day, in addition to the traditional publishers with staff of professional writers and editors who maintain established standards and are accountable to their readers, subscribers, paid sponsors, and shareholders. Today, we describe the aggregate of content being published in terms of data, or data bytes, or "Big Data" for the enormous amount of content that we produce, store, and retrieve. Like our national debt, the amount of data that is generated in the English language alone is impossible to be captured and communicated in a way that any one of us mere mortals could truly grasp.

According to DOMO, a technology company specializing in cloud-based business intelligence tools, over "2.5 quintillion bytes of data are created every single day, and it's only going to grow from there. By 2020, it is estimated that 1.7MB of data will be created every second for every person on earth."[2] I cannot comprehend how many files, books, articles, and posts we can collectively create by having quintillions of bytes available to use on our computer storage drives. With 18 zeroes—1,000,000,000,000,000,000— six more than a trillion, or a million trillion, a quintillion is impossible for me to conceptualize. Perhaps slightly easier to comprehend, but mind-blowing nonetheless, is that 90% of all data in the world has been generated over the last two years.[3]

How much of that "data" is of any use, or anyone cares about, is a different question, but included is everything from the ridiculous to the sublime— from Instagram posts to Bob Dylan's catalog of songs. Shakespeare's plays are in the first 10%, which gives us some idea of how little content was produced over the last half millennium compared with the past three decades; or said another way, how much worthless stuff is being produced today. We can only hope that the next *King Lear* will emerge from the quintillions of data orbiting in cyberspace at any given moment.

Digital first, but not last

Almost all content that we produce and publish today is created digitally, stored on servers, and generally easy to retrieve. Except for legacy publications created prior to the widespread use of digital technology, it is no longer necessary to scan copies of print, reproduce printed materials onto microfilm or microfiche, or archive celluloid film to preserve our most favored content for posterity. Adopted by the newspaper industry in 2017, and generally embraced by most publishers today, a "digital first" principle recommends that all content and communications be created first in a

DATA, METADATA, AND HUMANS   55

digital format to use on electronic devices, and then repurposed, if desired, for print or other medium.

When accessible as a digital file, most content types can be used in a variety of formats, retrieved by several different types of electronic devices, translated into other languages, transmitted anywhere in the world, repurposed in part or whole, and stored for future use. We are not 100% certain that the digital files that we create today will be accessible 500 years from now as newer technologies make older ones obsolete, but for more than a decade, multiple global efforts have been underway to optimize digital files—alongside the initiatives to digitize and preserve legacy analog media (books, journals, newspapers, documents, film)—for perpetual archival storage.[4]

Although the amount of data that has been generated over the past few decades and continues to be created every day sounds staggering, the rapid pace of the growing quantity of digital information is not something that we need to consider slowing down. A hypothetical conclusion that too much content is being produced prompts the question: "Too much to whom?"— since any determination regarding the value of a selected data set would be entirely subjective; one person's food is another person's poison. And since the generation of digital content does not necessitate chopping down trees to make trillions of physical books, building warehouses for storing them, or erecting towering libraries for shelving them, it does not matter how much digital content we produce, or how big proprietary databases or the Internet grow. The cost of digital storage is relatively low, and the content that is uploaded to servers occupies a tiny fraction of the physical space as the same content would in print form. What matters is whether we can find what we are looking for. If there is an efficient way to locate the content that we know is housed in a particular database, the amount of content is irrelevant, and by searching for it, we would not even be aware of how little or how much content there is in total. We just need to be able to find the proverbial needle in the haystack quickly, any time we want and from any location.

In most cases, the information or content we would be interested in at any given moment probably exists, and has been stored somewhere, either in a database on a free website or behind a paywall. If we look in the right place, chances are we can find what we need, thanks to the metadata associated with that content. Metadata is akin to a Global Positioning

System (GPS) for digital content. If a digital asset—an article, book, photo, illustration, video, or product profile—is tagged (with a keyword, term, classification) accurately, i.e., has metadata correlated to it in a database, it can be found by means of a search engine. How successful we are at locating the asset depends on the size of the database, the quality of the metadata, the competitive assets that may have overlapping metadata, and how broad or narrow we make our search. If a book has a unique title and author and we enter this information in the search box of the electronic card catalog of a library, we should find it quickly if the book is in the library's collection in at least one format. However, if we search only for the book's genre, "novel," for example, the results we receive will include all the novels in the library's database, which could take some time to sift through. "Author," "title," and "genre" are typical (minimum) tags, or metadata, generally associated with a book. The library may have a print, digital, audio version or all three, but with the right metadata all editions of the book should appear in a list of search results.

When distributing their books through online partners, like Amazon, Hive (U.K.), or Booktopia (Australia) for retail sales, or Ingram for the academic and public library market, publishers submit a database of their titles along with the metadata associated with each title. Usually, each distributor will have their own "form" for entering the metadata, which can be an Excel worksheet or other common database software. Alternatively, publishers can enter their metadata into the ONIX database, which centralizes metadata that gets sent automatically to the publishers' partner distributors.[5] The various input fields that comprise the metadata for each one of a publisher's titles generates a kind of fingerprint for that title and enables it to be discovered among the hundreds of thousands, or millions of titles in the distributor's database. Standard metadata includes, at a minimum, a product code, indicating whether the book is a paperback, hardback, board book, e-book, audiobook, etc.; author; title; content description, or abstract; BISAC subject codes[6]; keywords; number of pages; suggested retail price; one or more barcode numbers—ISBN (International Standard Book Number), EAN (European Article Number), UPC (Universal Product Code)—and other identifying information depending on the distributor's guidelines. Amazon has their own guidelines for submitting metadata, which allows for at least six keywords to help target a search, and their own identification system, ASIN (Amazon Standard Identification

Number). The barcode numbers are unique to each product version, so using it to conduct a search should return only one result. For example, the ISBN 978-0553103540 (actual) signifies just one product: The hardcover first edition of *A Game of Thrones* (*Song of Ice and Fire*) by George R.R. Martin, published by Bantam. Each format of this same title—audiobook, paperback, mass market paperback, or multimedia CD-ROM—has its own unique ISBN, which is the equivalent of the book's DNA.

Accurate and complete metadata help titles appear at or near the top of search results when readers are looking for a book in a general subject category (like "imaginative fiction") as opposed to a specific title (*A Game of Thrones: [Song of Ice and Fire]*). By submitting detailed metadata for each of its titles, a publisher improves the odds that a reader will find one of its titles over a competitor's. For example, when a publisher releases a new paperback book for young adults, both in English and in a Spanish translation, to their online distributor, some of the metadata will be identical, like the author and the product code "BC," which signifies "paperback" in one distributor's form. The BISAC codes for both language editions will have a "YA" as a prefix to indicate that the book's subject matter best suits the "young adult" market; but one edition will have "ENG" and the other "SPA" in the language field. The bigger the database, the more useful this type of data is in helping readers find books that match their interests.

Behind the paywall

Structured data (i.e., digital content with metadata) will be far easier to find than unstructured or semi-structured data in any database regardless of size. Today, preparing metadata should be an automatic step in a publisher's workflow, and depending on the number of titles and formats that a publisher releases annually, managing, and compiling metadata—and submitting the files to distributors—can be a full-time job for someone in the company. But preparing metadata was not always a standard workflow function. So, although a publisher's front-list titles will likely have detailed metadata, its legacy titles may have semi-structured metadata or no metadata at all. Publishers that have built their databases over a long time or have acquired a list of titles—or an entire imprint—from another publisher often will discover inconsistencies in how the metadata for each title has been prepared, which can negatively affect sales if titles cannot be easily discovered in a search. Any publisher that has acquired several different outside lists will have a laborious manual task creating uniformity in the metadata across all titles.

As the Co-Founder and COO of Yewno, a content-mapping technology company that engages artificial intelligence (AI) to aid publishers by making their content as discoverable as possible to end-users, Ruth Pickering partners with researchers, academic institutions, libraries, and companies with large databases to make it easier to search and locate specific information among a large repository of various types of content. Ruth recognized a common problem with out-of-date, incomplete, inconsistent, irrelevant, or missing metadata in proprietary databases and launched Yewno to address it. Yewno's technology taps into a database to discover contextual information that may be hidden in a vast sea of semi-structured or unstructured data. Ruth describes how Yewno helped a university press make many more of their slow-selling, or no-selling, titles accessible to customers without manually going into the database and updating or improving the metadata, which would have been a daunting task:

> As anyone in publishing can tell you, there is growing evidence that enhanced semantic metadata drives sales. We wanted to test this theory in the real world, so we applied our AI technology to optimize the metadata around a portion of one university press's collection. The results were impressive. This press has several thousand titles in its database, and over the past 20 years, they had migrated their backlist titles across four separate mapping systems before introducing BISAC [Book Industry Standards and Communication] codes. The result was that most of these titles had only one BISAC code, and most of those were either out of date, or worse, not necessarily relevant to the content of the book. None had the more recently introduced keywords and abstracts pertinent to their fields, putting them at a significant disadvantage in today's online marketplace.

The publisher considered some of their older titles virtually undiscoverable and basically incapable of monetization. To update the metadata would have taken their staff an unfathomable amount of time to categorize—assuming that they were able to do it at all. So, they turned to Yewno to apply AI technology to not only raise those titles to the surface, but also to optimize their categorization in such a way as to make them marketable again. We selected 100 titles where there were no external factors that would impact the results. The outcome was a two- to seven-fold increase in sales over the next six months.

A frequent issue that Yewno helped to resolve while repairing the metadata was disambiguating subject terms in some of the semi-structured titles. Without clearly articulated metadata, some of the search terms would retrieve irrelevant results. Certain subject nouns that could have more than one meaning depending on the context in which they were used required additional cues to indicate what the article was about. A standard example that computer scientists and linguists use to demonstrate this ambiguity problem is the word "triangle," which could refer to a three-sided geometric shape, a musical instrument, or a social relationship among three parties. Without clarifying metadata, articles or book titles on any of these subjects could randomly come up in a database search using the same search term.

In doing their work with the university press's database, Yewno discovered titles in different disciplines with "envelope" as the subject, which could refer to the common device for sending a letter, a surrounding organic structure in biology, a radio wave, or a geometric curve. Yewno's AI technology was able to clarify the contextual meaning of all terms using artificial intelligence algorithms, which read the titles in the database and the full text algorithmically—this groups terms based on similar content in a knowledge graph—creating "topical hierarchies" that clearly disambiguated the various meanings of the terms by organizing them into their appropriate categories, and inserting a clarifying definition, or abstract.

As "Space" occurred frequently in the database for subject categories as disparate as "Aeronautics" and "Language Arts," Yewno's artificial intelligence created the following metadata to help locate the most relevant articles for the search term "Space":

Table 3.1 Search Term: Space

Term	Topic Hierarchy	Definition
Space	Philosophy/ontology	Space is the boundless three-dimensional extent in which objects and events have relative position and direction. Physical space is often conceived in three linear dimensions, although modern physicists usually consider it, with time, to be part of a boundless four-dimensional . . .
NASA (space)	Technology & engineering, aeronautics & astronautics, physics/astrophysics	The National Aeronautics and Space Administration (NASA) is an independent agency of the executive branch of the U.S. federal government responsible for the civilian space program, as well as aeronautics and aerospace research.
Outer space	Physics/astrophysics, technology & engineering, aeronautics & astronautics	Outer space or just space, is the void that exists between celestial bodies, including Earth. It is not completely empty, but consists of a hard vacuum containing a low density of particles, predominantly a plasma of hydrogen and helium as well as electromagnetic radiation, magnetic fields, . . .
Space (punctuation)	Language arts/composition & creative writing, computers & computer science/information systems	In writing, a space ( ) is a blank area that separates words, sentences, syllables (in syllabification), and other written or printed glyphs (characters). Conventions for spacing vary among languages, and in some languages, the spacing rules are complex.
Address space	Computers & computer science/system administration	In computing, an address space defines a range of discrete addresses, each of which may correspond to a network host, peripheral device, disk sector, a memory cell or other logical or physical entity. For software programs to save and retrieve stored data, each unit of data must have an address . . .
Space shuttle	Technology & engineering, aeronautics & astronautics	A partially reusable rocket-launched vehicle, a space shuttle is designed to go into orbit around Earth, to transport people and cargo to and from orbiting spacecraft, and to glide to a runway landing on its return to the Earth's surface.
European Space Agency	Technology & engineering, aeronautics & astronautics, social science/developing & emerging countries	European Space Agency (ESA), French Agence Spatiale Européenne (ASE), European space and space-technology research organization founded in 1975 from the merger of the European Launcher Development Organization (ELDO) and the European Space Research Organization (ESRO), . . .

Accurate and comprehensive metadata enables publishers to monetize their content by making their intellectual property—whether it consists of articles, books, or other media—more discoverable to the user. The metadata gives users a clear path to what they are looking for. A good search engine will only be as good as the quality of the metadata. By being cognizant of this, publishers can devote the same care inputting their metadata as they do to creating the article or book titles themselves.

Having quality metadata solves half the goal of making content discoverable. The other half depends on whether a publisher's content is available free on the Web or behind a paywall. Publishers do not always have to choose one model over the other, since both paths have their pros and cons, which we will discuss in Chapter 9. In either case, the preparation of the metadata does not change. However, unless the content from a free site is of a specific nature, it will compete with other content sources for the same traffic, and the competition increases the more general the subject matter. Publishers of health and finance information will have less competition than, say, travel or sports publishers. In this case, the publishers must amplify the ability of their metadata to rise in a search results page with marketing strategies like search engine optimization (SEO) and search engine marketing (SEM). Whether on a free and open website or behind a paywall on a proprietary site, the key starting point for publishers to attract the most amount of traffic, and to ensure that users find their content, is well structured data.

In addition to quality metadata for making sure that their titles are discoverable, publishers also must be in the right place at the right time, which means being able to establish awareness on their own, calling attention to their website, building their presence with marketing initiatives, or partnering with a distributor who has built scale and brand awareness by aggregating content from a variety of providers. A publisher also has the option of being part of a library service where patrons can get access to the product for free via the school, university, or public library's subscription. It is much like being in the role of a movie producer and deciding on whether a feature will be available for free on Netflix or HBO, or for an additional fee on an aggregator's site like Xfinity, Hulu, or Amazon Prime.

Because the Internet is free and accessible with a few keystrokes and single click of the mouse, most users have a "Google reflex," and tend to go there first to look something up or find content and do not look first to proprietary websites. Up until recently, even most university students would do their research by going to the Web, even though they might be missing out on much more relevant and accurate websites that they have access to for free through their university. In fact, in seminars that I went to in the early 2000s, academics claimed that only 94% of their faculty and student body went to Google first instead of their library's subscription websites.

But this trend is changing. Although most students reflexively go to Google first, the percentage of students who use their library resources as their initial step in conducting research is now closer to 40%.[7] Although the total amount of information free on the Web dwarfs what is available behind paywalls, that is not the case regarding specialized and scholarly information. According to a recently published article in *Research Involvement and Engagement*, paywalls remain common for scholarly journals, especially in medical research. They estimated that only 28% of all scholarly publications are available through open access, the rest being available by subscription only.[8] The data showed that there were large variations depending on the discipline—only 7% of pharmacy publications were available on open access while 58% of articles on global health research were open. Similar patterns can be found in other scholarly pursuits as well. My brother, who is an oncological surgeon, confirms that this is the case with medical research articles. He says that most of the journals he needs, reads, and contributes to are available through aggregators like PubMed, which taps into the MEDLINE database, provides abstracts for articles for free, but permits full-text access through institutional subscriptions only. Some of the most prestigious journals, like the *New England Journal of Medicine*, *Lancet*, or the *Journal of Clinical Oncology* can only be subscribed to directly.

Publishers need to make a business decision whether their content will live behind a paywall on an aggregator's site, is free on the Web, or is available only from the publisher's site and selective digital distributors. Whatever the publisher decides, the content should have accurate, comprehensive metadata so that it can be easily discovered wherever a user goes to retrieve it.

Notes

1. Although e-books became a widely accepted format only in the mid-1990s, Michael S. Hart, the founder of Project Gutenberg, is credited with having produced the first e-book as far back as 1971. Project Gutenberg is an

ongoing initiative to digitize and make available free to the public literary and other works that have passed into the public domain. Currently, they have 60,000 free e-books on their website.
2. This figure came from their website, domo.com, on February 11, 2021, so apparently, they too have a hard time keeping current with the data.
3. This is from *Science News*, May 22, 2013, so it is out of date. It is likely that the percentage has increased even more in the last 11 years, and over a shorter time. Still, it makes the point simply fine.
4. One of many digital preservation efforts takes place at the Packard Campus for Audio-Visual Conservation, a branch of the Library of Congress, in Culpepper, Virginia. Its mission includes the conversion of film to digital files, the development of sustainable digital file formats, structured metadata, and digital file storage, activities it has been undertaking since 2008. I describe my visit to the facility in the Epilogue to this book.
5. ONIX, an acronym for the Online Information Exchange, is a database for metadata aggregators developed by EDItEUR, an international organization that promotes standards for the global book and e-book trade.
6. BISAC (Book Industry Standards and Communications) codes are a list of subjects designed for use in the book trade in the U.S. and English-Speaking Canada created and maintained by the Book Industry Study Group (BISG), founded in 1975 by the Book Manufacturers Institute.
7. Data from *College & Research Libraries*, Vol. 77, No. 5, "Undergraduates' Use of Google vs. Library Resources: A Four-Year Cohort Study," © 2016 Carrol Perruso.
8. This data is from "Open to the public: Paywalls and the public rationale for open access medical research publishing," Research Involvement and Engagement, Suzanne Day, et al., Article number 8, February 17, 2020; © 2021 BioMed Central Ltd.

4

EDTECH

Closing the digital divide

> Everybody gets so much information all day long that they lose their common sense.
>
> —**Gertrude Stein**

The publishing community knows more about the content and resource needs of the K-12 education market than it does about almost any other market, thanks in large part to two factors: Transparency, or the easy access to sector data, including student enrollment numbers, annual budgets, and curriculum requirements around standards; and the close relationship between publishing executives and stakeholders in education—state and district superintendents, CEOs of the largest school districts, principals, chief academic officers, department directors, teachers, and librarians. Leaders from both sectors meet regularly at various industry-sponsored events or through non-profit organizations to share insights about student success and teacher engagement; discuss roadblocks to achieving academic goals; assess the relative merits of educational trends; and brainstorm on

DOI: 10.4324/9781003162636-5

how to create better learning environments and effective pedagogical materials for teachers and students.

Even though the functional relationship between publishers and educators is one of vendor and buyer, interdependent objectives provide incentives for both parties to collaborate—educators have a mandate to motivate students to master the subject matter and improve their critical thinking skills, while publishers assist that effort by organizing, packaging, and delivering standards-aligned content in accessible and appealing formats.

Over the past 40 years, I have been an active member of or have participated in events sponsored by several of the organizations established to promote the collaboration between publishers—especially EdTech publishers—and educators. Some of these organizations include the Education Research & Development Institute (ERDI), the International Society for Technology in Education (ISTE), the Consortium for School Networking (CoSN), the State Educational Technology Directors Association (SETDA), and Digital Promise, all of which organize meetings with publishers and educators to encourage innovation and help educators find ways to leverage technology and close the digital divide that exists in our society. I have also been on the board, serving a term as president, of the Association of Educational Publishers (AEP), now part of the Association of American Publishers (AAP), where we sought to understand how, in concert with the education community, we could democratize learning and level the playing field for educators and students across the 13,600 school districts in the United States.

The ambitious goals of these organizations and others like them attest to the high priority being allotted to the successful implementation of the latest technology in every school. Since the introduction of educational films and filmstrips and overhead projectors into classrooms, employing technology to enhance the curriculum—bringing learning to life and igniting students' imagination—has been challenging. With the explosion of digital solutions and the personalization of technology, as well as the imperative to provide the training necessary to empower teachers to inspire classrooms of digital natives, the challenges have become even greater, making the work of education and publishing partnerships more essential than ever.

Byte-sized learning

The extent to which technology is being used in schools varies by grade, from state to state, and district to district. Since any technology implementation today depends on connectivity to the Internet and minimum technology requirements in schools and homes, economic discrepancies among families from district to district and even within a district make it difficult for educational leaders to devise a consistent strategy that is both workable and equitable. For years school leaders in most districts across the country have tried to develop a technology strategy that eschews economic inequalities, but uneven and limited school budgets make that difficult to achieve. Even if most schools have adequate connectivity, some homes may not have an Internet connection at all, or any computing device other than a smartphone, and sometimes not even one of those. This means that technology-based courseware solutions either as primary course work or for homework cannot be universally required since that would put some students at a severe disadvantage.

The situation is quite different in higher education, where digital learning is the norm, and has been for quite some time. Students and faculty do most of their class management work, including assignments and readings, in learning management systems (LMS) and specialized digital platforms. Textbooks, to the extent that they are still used, are accessed online or as a digital download. My son, who is graduating from Northwestern in June, has not purchased a print textbook for any of his classes during his four years as a student. And that was true for the past two years of his sister's career at Emory, where she graduated from in 2019. Most of the publishers in higher education generate most of their revenue from digital content. Overall, higher education publishers in the United States receive more than 75% of their revenue from digital products and licenses. In contrast, even in the high school segment of the K-12 market—except for the most progressive and well-funded districts and private schools—usage of digital solutions is far less than what it is in higher education.

Still, investment in EdTech over the past decade has been aggressive by any standard; big bets from venture capital and private equity are being made on technology-driven solutions for education, driving up valuations of late-stage EdTech startups. According to Thomas Dee, a professor at Stanford University's Graduate School of Education and a senior fellow at the Stanford Institute for Economic Policy Research, venture capital investment in education technology during 2020 exceeded $9.7 billion, twice the amount spent in 2019, and largely going to online learning platforms.[1] The global investment landscape in education is also robust. According to a recent London & Partners report, the estimated value of London's EdTech ecosystem is $3.4 billion, while global EdTech VC investment was on track to grow by 15% in 2020 to $7.6 billion.[2] In short, there is overwhelming optimism in the investment community that EdTech will continue to be a strong growth area and will play an increasingly larger role in K-12 and higher education.

Meanwhile, the enthusiasm and significant investment in EdTech comes face to face with a palpable global digital divide. In the United States, the 131,000 K-12 schools fall within a spectrum from little or occasional use of technology up to fully implemented 1:1 computer-to-student ratios. According to recent government-sponsored and private reports on the K-12 market, barriers to technology implementation are primarily economic, not ideological; few educators are against wider use of technology and would want to spend more time with it if they had the funds and the devices.

Teachers' viewpoints on the state of technology integration in their respective schools vary widely. At the low end, where the building's Internet speeds are too slow for productive work, it is often faster for students to use their phones. Here are some comments from teachers in schools with a range of technology implementation from low to high.[3]

Table 4.1 K-12 Teacher Comments

"We have devices to share between multiple classrooms (laptops). We have a printing budget and are encouraged to go digital with our materials, but we don't have the tech to support this vision."
"I have a cart of (25) Chromebooks, a cart of (20) iPads, and a computer lab of outdated desktop computers."
"All students are provided a Lenovo Yoga laptop, but 1/3 of them do not work properly or have so much 'security-ware' that they run too slow, and many students leave them in their lockers and use their phones."
"All students have school-issued Chromebooks. Most, if not all, students also have smartphones. We also have a Smartboard that accesses the Internet and can be used for presentations."
"At my school, each student has a Chromebook. Each classroom has a projector, and most have an iPad."
"I'm fortunate. My school is 1:1 iPad. The cameras are not turned on for the students. The students have a district app store, so the apps they can use are limited. Teachers all have interactive whiteboards, doc cameras, and microphones."

"Teachers Talk Technology," MDR Insights: State of the K-12 Market 2018, © Copyright 2018 MDR.

Given the choice, teachers would opt for more technology in their schools, and more digital resources, especially from the middle school on up. Most teachers believe that technology improves education and has enabled student agency by allowing students to take ownership over their learning, explore their own personal interests in more depth, and recognize authoritative sources as opposed to trusting information simply because it was presented to them in textbooks.

Educators and publishers share a vision and a goal—to achieve 1:1 computer-to-student learning in all 131,000 K-12 schools in the United States. Although the timeline for achieving that goal is not fixed, some steps are being taken to pick up the pace, even if in some districts they seem like baby steps. For example, regarding student assessment, all students can now be tested electronically. Because most schools have at least one computer in the classroom and are able to share computers for temporary use with mobile computer carts,[4] student assessment is generally done entirely online. As a result, according to the National Center for Education Statistics (NCES), "to address the increased role of technology in classrooms, [the Center] is transitioning the National Assessment of Educational Progress (NAEP) from paper and pencil to digital assessments."[5] This represents progress on a national scale, but it is still a long way from being able to exploit digital curriculum on a regular basis in every classroom.

Within K-12, high school classes employ the most technology, especially in schools that send more than 85% of their graduates on to colleges and universities. Many middle school courses have been transitioning to digital solutions as well, and teachers are receptive to replacing print-based products with digital solutions wherever they can add more flexibility and better value. However, many K-5 teachers, even if they can use technology equitably across their student population, still have a strong preference for print, though they see the benefits of having some digital components accessible to provide additional support, interactivity, and engagement. Overall, elementary-level teachers favor a blended solution of both print and digital materials and are not inclined to move to all-digital products. Here is how that preference was confirmed by one publisher and client of Ross & Associates:

Last summer, I consulted with a K-8 publisher that has been the leader in their subject category for more than 40 years. Their best-selling product, representing 65% of their total revenue, and more

than 70% of their profit, is a boxed set of print components with online teacher support materials and training videos. They had already ceased updating the middle-school version of the same program and had successfully replaced it with an all-digital version. After only two years in the market, it was the fastest-growing product in their catalog.

Based on this success, the company's management planned to develop a digital product for grades K-5 as well. But they had two concerns: While they did not want to cannibalize the sales of their highest gross-selling product, they also did not want to risk losing market share to a competitor who might come out with an all-digital product, especially if the market in general was ready to make the switch from print. They asked me and my team to determine how receptive the market would be to an all-digital K-5 product and at what price point, thinking that it would be better for them to cannibalize themselves than have someone else do it for them.

Fortunately, they had a large database of current and prospective customers that we were able to survey and interview and who were eager to provide feedback. We received more than enough responses to generate a 96% reliability rating on the survey. In addition, the difference in the responses between their existing customers and prospects turned out to be statistically insignificant, which further confirmed the reliability of the data. The survey recipients were restricted to decision makers or staff members involved in the decision-making process, which included superintendents, principals, curriculum directors, counselors, teachers, and librarians. Given three choices—print only, digital only, or a hybrid product that combined both print and digital—three-quarters of the respondents felt that the print-digital hybrid product would be of greater value than the all-digital product.

With the middle-school market, however, only 15% of the respondents favored a print-only product and more than half thought that an all-digital product would be of greater value than a hybrid product. Based on these results, the publisher received the reinforcement that they expected for replacing the print product with an all-digital version at the middle-school product level and determined with a high degree of confidence that they should move forward with an all-digital K-5 program while continuing to sell and update their existing print version.

The education market is not monolithic; what may be a preference in one district may not be in another. The variance from district to district and from state to state means publishers must rely on both fresh data and educated guesswork to make product development decisions. Just because one district has mandated that they will purchase only all-digital curriculum in some subjects, does not mean that all districts in the state will follow suit.

Nineteen states are so-called "adoption states," meaning that they establish statewide requirements for the curriculum and determine which programs successfully meet those requirements. They also provide the funds for purchasing the products. With minor exceptions, only programs that are approved can be purchased with state funds.[6] Some of the largest adoption states, like Texas, Florida, and California, rotate statewide adoptions in math, science, language arts, and social studies, typically on six- or seven-year cycles.

Given the value and infrequency of the adoptions, they have an outsized influence on the product development priorities of the publishers who choose to participate in them. Because of the generally inconsistent use of technology throughout a state, up until recently state officials have been reluctant to shift their essential adoption requirements away from primarily print-based products. Technology components that were included in their adoption guidelines were supplemental to the main print components. However, the trend is changing, and now states are approving both all-digital and print-based products if they meet the curriculum requirements. Yet publishers have concerns that with the variation in technology readiness, the larger districts in the largest states may have a bias against all-digital submissions if some schools do not have the technology in place to take advantage of technology-dependent programs. Recently a client of Ross & Associates had to address this concern with one of their best-selling programs:

Three years ago, California had put out an RFP for K-12 science programs, and for the first time in the science adoption cycle, they opened it up to all-digital products on all levels. In other words, state funding would be available to use for any program that a district chose that was on the approval list regardless of format. After all the evaluations were completed, the state approved more than two dozen submissions. A variety of multi-grade and all-grade print only, all-digital, and hybrid products were approved. As a standard practice, all the approved programs were made available on a website for viewing to help districts decide which programs to select.

One of the approved all-digital programs was developed by a potential client of mine, and although they were pleased to have made the adoption list, their sales team was nervous that many schools would not purchase a program without any printed materials. The program did allow downloading of PDF materials from the website, but the sales team, still, was concerned that would not be enough, particularly if schools did not have access to printers or have a large enough budget to print out materials for every student when needed.

There was no way of knowing in advance how districts would behave when decision-time came around, so to remove any possible obstacles to making a sale, the publisher decided to also provide bound printed versions of all student and teacher materials in the program, which meant designing, editing, composing, and ultimately going to press with 13 student books and teachers' editions. It was an expensive insurance policy or hedge against a district rejecting their program if some of their schools were not sufficiently tech ready. I am not sure how well they did in the adoption, but they will never know if they would have achieved the same level of sales had they not added the printed editions as part of the offering.

Once purchased, the same adoption materials are used for 5–7 years depending on the state's adoption cycle. If the curriculum is available online as a license, the publisher will revise and improve it over the adoption period. But the printed materials do not change or get revised and are likely to be out of date and in need of revision halfway through the adoption cycle. In the example above, if a school had purchased the printed books and licensed the online version, the two formats would grow farther apart over time as revisions were made to the online version and the print components remain stagnant. Worse yet, even after the adoption cycle, some districts, because of budget shortfalls, tend to continue using the same materials past what might be considered their "expiration date." In some cases, students may be using materials that are as old as they are. It is difficult to motivate students when they lose trust in aging or outdated materials, which should be an incentive for schools to move to digital solutions. I experienced first-hand how long a district might continue using the components of a print-based program after a district-wide adoption:

I was working for a publisher who had produced a new middle-school math program a few years prior to my arrival at the company that was adopted by a large metropolitan city on the east coast. The city had placed the program in each of its middle schools and had tracked the yearly progress that their students had made on standardized tests since implementing the program. After five years, the normal cycle for an adoption in their state, they discovered that students using the program performed 50% better on standardized math tests than districts using other programs. We assumed that with this kind of success, the city would upgrade to the second edition of the program when math came up again in the adoption cycle, which was in two years.

The second edition was a major overhaul of the program. Even though it utilized the same basic pedagogical methodology for teaching math as the first edition, the second edition was in full color, had all new artwork and photography, revealed more diversity in the real-life situations that middle schoolers would relate to, and most crucially was aligned to the common core standards, which was a requirement for adoptions in most districts.

Due to cuts in the city's budget, the district opted not to purchase the second edition but replaced books from the first edition that had been damaged or lost. Even when we had published a third edition of the series five years later, the city continued using the edition they had. By this time, students were using 12-year-old books that were not only partially in black and white, but had math problems with gasoline, clothing, and grocery prices that were obsolete. Because they were no longer current customers, I lost track of how recent students were performing with the original program, but I did not see published results of an upward trend. In terms of the math program's trajectory, the last edition we produced was entirely digital.

Digital finds a platform

When schools purchase textbooks or printed materials, they own them. And because they are expensive, districts tend to extend their use for as long as possible, even as books become out of date, and especially when budgets are tight. For example, instead of buying a new edition of a math program at the end of an adoption period, a school district or state may choose to keep the existing program and use their budget to purchase a new language arts, social studies, science, or STEM program. But by continuing to put off replacing aging products, their entire curriculum suite risks becoming out of date. However, digital products are licensed, not purchased, and have the advantage of being continually revised (which is the commitment that a publisher makes with the license) and more economical when the two formats are compared on an annual basis.

Let us go through a hypothetical scenario to see how this might play out. A new basal textbook series might cost $80 for each student edition. The teacher's edition normally costs 50% more than that but let us leave that out of the equation for this exercise. Workbooks, journals, practice assessments, and other consumable print products would cost extra, and these would normally have to be replaced every year for new incoming students—let us assign a very conservative $8 per student per year for those items. Textbooks would have optional extension materials that students could access online, including additional readings or exercises, graphic organizers, interactivities, and maybe videos. Access to the program's website would come at an extra charge, let us say $6.00 per student per year. This print-plus version, over five years, would end up costing the school approximately $30 per student per year, and for the last few years of the adoption cycle, students would have been using an outdated textbook. For approximately the same annual cost, the school could have a license to an all-digital product, with every component available online but with the option to print out materials if they wished. And every new incoming class would have up-to-date content to work from. In addition, an online curriculum product would come with other time-saving functionality that would be of great value to the teacher and district, like a dashboard for tracking student progress, assigning homework, lesson planning, and measuring student outcomes.

Depending on how many additional years a school decides to lengthen the use of a textbook, they might be able to save some money on the cost per student after 6 or 7 years, but they put their students and teachers at a disadvantage. And because teachers must supplement older material, they might have to spend their own time or money to bring in current information, which would be hidden costs not accounted for in the school budget. In addition, once they do decide to replace the books, the schools have "brown bananas" to dispose of.

With more exposure to digital products and the functionality that they provide, more districts are realizing the value of licensing digital products and services over purchasing print products that become out of date and somewhat of an embarrassment. Districts may be able defend switching to digital products if they look at their budgets differently. Instead of spending most of their allotment the first year, they might amortize their costs over time; a $100 purchase of a textbook would be equivalent to licensing a digital product at $10 per student per year for ten years.

Although an element of guesswork will always be part of determining whether an educational product will ultimately succeed, and what format schools are likely to favor, there are trends that light the way. In the case of digital products, particularly at the middle-school level and above, the market appears to be pegging its success on Learning Management Systems (LMS) or Learning Management Content Systems (LMCS). Other than e-book downloads, digital products are accessed from cloud-based platforms, which have been built uniquely for a particular product, or customized from a "white-label" platform licensed from a software company, rebranded, and used as a "container" for the publisher's product. Either way, they are password-protected hosted solutions. As a district accumulates multiple licenses of online products, it can become cumbersome to manage the various passwords, particularly when many of the products that they use provide individual student and teacher access with unique credentials. To simplify this, and to accomplish several other objectives, districts can adopt one of the many available LMS platforms, which allow for single sign-on (SSO), giving users access to all the products licensed by the school through one online portal.

When adopting an LMS platform, schools consider several needs: Integrating licensed web content; integrating other third-party content that they may have on their servers; uploading previously created student and teacher content like photos and videos, and perhaps thousands of other resources and digital files that they may have accumulated over the years, such as lesson plans, pacing guides, public domain e-books, photos, and creative work. All this digital data can be gathered, stored in the LMS, and accessed for repurposing. The LMS becomes the central portal for taking advantage of the school's or district's investments made in digital content over the years, as well as providing access to current online subscriptions.

Efforts by districts to install LMS platforms have been ongoing for at least ten years and they are picking up steam. Some LMS platforms, like Google Classroom, are free; others can come with hefty licensing and implementation fees. Table 4.2 is a brief overview of what teachers like about using platforms. Not all platforms have all these features and benefits, and some are easier to implement than others, but the items in the figure represent a wish-list of sorts. Above all these is safety, which would be a chief requirement regardless of other values.

Table 4.2 LMS Features and Benefits

Features	Benefits
Grade book; student rostering	Save time: a key benefit for all teachers
Post notes; feedback	Track student progress
Post homework	Single sign-on: a key benefit for admin and teachers
Post assignments	Student self-check: giving students control
Manage content	Integrate third-party content: databases, journals, e-books, videos, photos, maximizing investment in content
Games	Import data, to have data in one repository
Ease of use	Integrate and edit curriculum
Record and post audio and video	Mobile
Stats and usage reports	Integrate standards: e.g., CCSS, NGSS, Lexiles,
Quiz editor	Personalize content
Dashboard	Share lesson plans
Adaptive study modes	Teachers and students can collaborate and communicate with peers.
Save content from each session	Free option: but sometimes this means free like a puppy, not like air. Paid LMS platforms come with support and editorial guidance and require less in-house expertise.

EdTech meets a real "bug"

Like it did for many aspects of our life, the Covid-19 pandemic disrupted the everyday routine of education and with it uncovered more opportunities for EdTech. Some of the trends were already clear and being implemented, but the pandemic certainly accelerated the use of technology. Overnight, teachers and students became more dependent on online products. With students and teachers out of the building and working remotely, virtual classes became the norm, and any "face-to-face" teaching had to be done via video chat, which meant crash courses in using Zoom or Google Meet. Educators had to quickly assess which lessons could be recorded and presented asynchronously and which ones had to be done synchronously. Teachers had to develop new strategies to engage students over a long virtual lesson or to hold their attention during webinars. Teacher training and educational conferences that were previously conducted live on site had to be re-engineered virtually.

Interactions that had to move from a physical to a virtual environment were not unique to schools. The issues that virtual teaching raised were no different from those that many other industries faced in trying to maintain normal business activities without being in the same physical space. But one consequence for education was a much greater than normal reliance on digital content, either through their school network, the library, or free websites. Before the pandemic, the trend, as we have been discussing throughout this book, was gravitating to online programs, e-books, digital platforms, and free content from non-profits like PBS and the BBC. If anything, the pandemic gave more value to online products and resources than they had before as online learning was promoted from a "nice-to-have" to a "must-have" status. But although teachers and students at all levels are eager to get back in the classroom when the pandemic is over, it is more than likely that online learning will take up an increasing amount of classroom time, and that some of the learning strategies that we used to adjust to the pandemic will become permanent. Also, over the last year, the educational technology industry has been given a boost from investors with more venture capital going to EdTech early-stage startups and heightened attention from private equity to late-stage startups with a substantial user base. With much enthusiasm around EdTech innovation, it is unlikely that we will return to the way things were—and more compelling reasons exist not to.

The adjustment to the new normal during the pandemic was easier for those schools and institutions that had already started down the road to more technology-centered teaching and learning. Here's how Lisa Schmucki, Founder and CEO of edWeb.net, an online webinar service, describes her role in supporting the EdTech community in making online education more engaging—before and during the pandemic:

Silos in education, especially the isolation of teachers in the classroom or school leaders in their buildings, have long been a major inhibition to better communication and collaboration between educators working in the profession; between educators and the creators and publishers of learning materials; between educators and the associations who advocate on their behalf. And now we have everyone isolated in their homes during a pandemic.

When social networking came along, I immediately saw this as an opportunity to break down the silos that exist across the education industry with online networking and collaboration. EdWeb.net was founded as a professional social and learning network in 2008. That was only the first step. The more important problem to solve was how to create a sustainable business model. Having worked in publishing for 30 years, I knew about the wealth of expertise and connections that education companies have access to with their authors, consultants, and customers. Why not ask these companies to tap into those resources to host free professional learning on the edWeb.net network? And in return, they would get great marketing content, insights, and leads.

We began integrating edWebinars, hosted by sponsors and partners, into topical social networking communities on edWeb, creating a highly successful, sustainable, and disruptive business model: Sponsors recruit and host innovative educators and experts to deliver high-quality professional learning; educators receive free professional learning on every topic imaginable from preK-12; and edWeb provides CE [continuing Education] certificates for educators who attend and view our programs—all for free. The edWeb CE credits are now accepted in 40 states for teacher re-licensure.

With edWeb, sponsors are recognized for their thought leadership and expertise, creating valuable brand recognition. The presentations are recorded and distributed in video, podcast, and print form, resulting in valuable marketing content. Sponsors also receive all the program registrants and attendees as leads. edWeb has succeeded in creating a new concept in marketing, "PD Marketing," and has created a new media channel to the market. During this time of Covid-19, this is more significant and important than ever.

Educators need the "PD" or professional learning support to cope with unprecedented challenges and change; edWeb delivers all this PD for free, disrupting the traditional professional development market—and at a much lower cost to sponsors, disrupting the education media market of hosting sponsored content.

EdWeb.net programs continue to grow in membership and sponsorship, especially in the wake of the Covid-19 pandemic. We now have nearly 1 million educators in our community and over 100 sponsors and partners. We provide all the professional learning and CE certificates for educators for free, and all the program logistics and marketing for sponsors, making it a turnkey and personalized marketing and lead generation program for the education companies and non-profits.

We get incredible comments from educators, sponsors, and presenters and post them on our website. It is very gratifying, especially at this time, to have created a disruptive new model that does so well and does so much good. Online education is now a must-have and not a nice-to-have. What work have we done so far to make this as useful as possible, and what is the next evolution?

Making the transition from the habitual model of classroom teaching to virtual teaching required an adjustment that no one was prepared for. Schools were familiar with fire drills, and over the last few years have gone through extensive training in case of the sudden appearance of a hostile intruder. But teachers and administrators did not conduct practice drills for "what-if" scenarios in case of a pandemic and everyone had to immediately turn to a virtual teaching model. Lynelle Morganthaler, VP of Learning Design at

Edmentum, an online test preparation publisher, describes how she helped teachers from traditional classroom environments make the transition with one curriculum product specially designed for virtual classrooms:

During the pandemic, we began selling a previously limited-market digital curriculum in high volumes to school districts. Prior to that point, it was largely used in virtual school implementations. As the product took hold in the public-school market, a lot of strange things began to happen.

First, schoolteachers forgot everything they knew about teaching in the classroom and were unable to use their face-to-face practices and create similar virtual practices. Then we began observing that schools believed that a digital curriculum, unlike a print curriculum, would teach all by itself. Parents seemed to have the viewpoint that a digital curriculum would magically keep their six-year-olds completely captivated for hours at a time. Some schools even reduced teaching staff to 1:50 ratios in K-2—something that would not be accepted for in-person learning in most states.

So, we set about creating materials—"A Day in the Life" guides—that helped reset expectations. Short welcome kits introduced teachers, students, and parents to their roles and the role of the curriculum, emphasizing the importance of teachers using a digital curriculum like the way they would use other instructional tools, such as a textbook.

The guides introduced teachers to an implementation model of what an instructional day during virtual learning might look like. From various anecdotes, teachers went through a lesson identifying expected student outcomes and matched them to the key lesson sections they needed to tackle in their synchronous online lessons. They identified lesson sections where small groups could better address individual needs, and independent activities with which students and their family learning guides could be expected to be successful. These models helped teachers adapt the techniques that they had used in their classrooms and apply them to the new paradigm of virtual instruction—which, as it turns out, does not need to look like uncharted territory if they have confidence in what they already know and can do well.

Even though EdTech companies were there to help educators during this tumultuous time and often went the extra mile, the general frustration level often ended up spilling over from educators and parents onto our teams. Resetting expectations through welcome kits and implementation toolkits was critical to helping everyone understand how educators could be successful, how we could best support them, and distinguishing between being frustrated with the pandemic and not with each other.

Training squeals

Training has never been a trivial part of a publisher's budget and it has become an even more significant piece of the deliverables that teachers and administrators expect to get from EdTech publishers. In talking to teachers, I have frequently heard training come up as top of mind. It is also a frequent topic for sales representatives, who are not only expected to be curriculum specialists but tech experts as well. It is impossible to consult with an educator on the value of a digital curriculum product without also being able to communicate the technology requirements for implementing it.

Publishers not only find themselves responsible for providing training on their own products but also general training on LMS platforms that their curriculum must integrate with as well as productivity tools, like Google Classroom, Google Forms, and Zoom, which often are provided free to schools—but without technical support, which means that they are free like a puppy. Technology can be overwhelming for even seasoned users, and it is more than likely that teachers, and sales representatives, can use fewer details on all possible functions that the technology can provide and more targeted training on what they need and are most likely to use over the course of the year. Generally, the simplest solutions are the most useful ones.

Vicki Smith Bigham, an education product development, training, and marketing consultant, has been training sales representatives and teachers for more than 40 years. Her suggestion, KISS—Keep It Simple, St***d:

For several years in the early to mid-1990s, I traveled nationwide training K-2 teachers on the use of an exciting new hardware and curriculum bundle of products. It was an extremely innovative and well-received set of materials. The training model was as excellent as the quality of the software and instructional materials. Training encompassed hardware orientation, introduction to a variety of software packages, integration strategies, classroom management, and modeling of classroom teaching, with return visits by the trainer spaced over months.

One of the largest purchases and installations was in a Houston-area suburb, and senior executives from the company offering the product were eager to conduct a site visit and hear firsthand what the teachers liked most and any additional support they might need to be successful. They came to a campus and observed classroom teaching and learning activities and then, at the end of the day, the teachers and executives all sat together in a room to debrief. And yes, they were sitting in kindergarten chairs!

The teacher-support materials provided were extensive—big binders of lessons and resources, templates and books, worksheets, posters to create interest and encourage use, strategies for individual and group work, and more. All the materials were professionally packaged in a large box with a beautiful design.

The executives began to eagerly ask what else they might provide. Videos of classroom teaching ideas? Online access to additional resources? Searchable data files of lesson topics? And the list grew.

After a few moments of silence, one teacher raised her hand to be called on and then responded, "Could we just have a recipe box with one concrete idea on each index card?"

I have never forgotten that experience and the reminder to spend as much attention on meeting teachers where they are and giving them what *they* will most value as we do on the glossy design and packaging of what we offer.

The way that publishers have conducted training in the past—either paid training for customers or training for sales representatives and in-house staff—has been disrupted and turned upside down due to the pandemic. Most paid customer training had been conducted in-person, which, since the pandemic, has shown up as a black hole on profit-and-loss sheets.

Publishers have had to create virtual training on the fly, both asynchronously and synchronously. In some cases, after some trial and error and free offerings, the revenue from virtual training has matched in-person training. Although there are costs associated with the development of videos and the distribution of the digital content on platforms through newly developed websites, publishers, and their customers, have saved on travel expenses by not sending trainers to on-site visits, and more customers can be trained in a shorter time by using technology. Although it has taken some getting used to, for the most part, both the publishers and their customers seem to agree that little is lost by going virtual with some tangible upsides.

The jury is out on whether in-person training will return to anything like it was before, but some publishers have already concluded that the forced change has been a boon, and that virtual training will save time and resources for themselves as well as for their customers; enable them to impact more customers more quickly; and provide the same, if not better, service than being on site.

Rachelle Cracchiolo, the Founder and CEO of Teacher Created Materials (TCM), a successful K-8 publisher, has emphasized the importance of training from the time she launched her company more than 40 years ago. Even though 90% of her sales today are still from print products—with only modest technology add-ons for her customers to master—training has always been a primary differentiator for the company, and a key to her success.

I was on Rachelle's board of advisors for seven years, and she would always stress in board meetings that in addition to creating products by "teachers and for teachers," a key selling point and TCM's special sauce was "teaching teachers how to teach"—and teaching sales reps how to sell. To make good on this mission, the company devoted significant resources to bringing teachers into the company headquarters in Huntington Beach, California, regularly for in-person training sessions, and held sales conferences there twice a year at substantial expense. Yet, due to the pandemic and being forced to conduct all training virtually, Rachelle says she will never go back to training her sales force or her customers in the same way again. Here is a bulleted list of key results on what has changed for TCM and why the new normal is Rachelle's new status quo:

- **Overview:** Global meetings and conferences, whether for company training or professional development for customers, reached a critical need since Covid-19. The roles of physical and virtual meetings and presentations have been turned on their heads.
- **Sales meetings:** Post pandemic, we will probably no longer have in-person annual or semi-annual sales meetings, which will result in hundreds of thousands of dollars of savings. Massive amounts of time will be saved as every individual no longer needs to spend money on plane fares and hotel stays, and the company saves additional money by not having to feed dozens and sometimes hundreds of salespeople. The last global sales conference we had virtually was the best sales meeting we ever had.
- **Board meetings:** These too no longer need to be live. Board members will still receive stipends, but large savings can be gained by foregoing three-day board meetings when two of those days could have involved travel—which is lost time for the board members at the company's expense.
- **Professional development:** If I don't teach teachers, you might as well set the products on fire. In one district in California, for example, without training we would have seen 1 million dollars of product sales go to waste because no one would have known how to use them. But how we did PD in the past is not how we are doing it now or how we are likely to do it in the future.
  - We have found that the price we charge for PD is the same online as it was in person; but over two days instead of three—and no travel expenses. It's a "10" for training teachers (and reps).
  - People can participate from different locations; no flying or driving. We can scale our training in a way that would not have been possible if we could not do it online. In one recent training session, we had 600 teachers online simultaneously.
- **Students/parents:** There is probably no better way to train students on how to benefit from distance learning than modeling it virtually. Luckily, we can involve our most popular authors, like Kwame Alexander, in online question-and-answer sessions. We had him on a 20-minute video, which was also attended by parents.

- We will recruit more famous teachers for virtual group meetings.
- **Focus groups:** Focus groups used to be very costly to arrange and conduct—renting meeting rooms in a single location, getting people to attend, paying for travel and expenses, setting up separate recording equipment, etc. Now we can have these irrespective of location, pay people for their attendance and contributions, and save everyone the time and expense of gathering in one spot.
- **Trade shows:** No more trade shows! They are expensive with a lot of down time. Most will go virtual, we suspect.
- **Strategies:** We are still learning. We have learned strategies that we can repeat to optimize the online experience, and we have stopped using some techniques that did not work.
  - We learned how to do online learning and in specific ways that could improve on live instruction. In some ways, we experienced better control with less distraction.
  - Virtual training can be personalized. We make good use of online break-out sections. Chat can be used to comment without interrupting the speakers. We get more participation. This is working well with the teachers, and out of 30 participants, we can usually count on two rising stars. By adding music, we can help enhance the environment.
  - In a session of 120 attendees, you end up with less than three minutes each, but everyone participates. The top reps will shine, and by being virtual, we aren't wining and dining reps that end up being unproductive in the field.

Successful publishers, who create long-term value for their customers, will take advantage of the opportunities that online training affords even though some of the advantages of in-person training cannot be duplicated. For customers, they should see training as an extension of the online experiences of the products themselves—if the training is good, the products should be as well. Even veteran teachers appreciate product training given the increasing dependency on technology and the reality of feature creep. Online products are not "open books," and their value reveals itself in a non-linear manner. Effective training can help teachers prioritize features that work best with their preferred methodologies.

Notes

1. "VCs Are Pouring Money into the Wrong Education Startups," *Wired*, January 28, 2020.
2. "London Leads European EdTech Revolution," *London & Partners*, September 7, 2020.
3. Quotes in the table have been selected from "Teachers Talk Technology," *MDR Insights: State of the K-12 Market 2018*, © Copyright 2018 Market Data Retrieval.
4. According to a recent MDR report, a typical K-12 classroom will have a teacher's desktop computer, classroom projector, interactive whiteboard, and use of a mobile computer cart. Well-funded schools have clickers (classroom response system) and provide Chromebooks, and sometimes iPads, for each student. "Insight Report: How 2020 Shifted Perceptions of Technology in the Classroom," ©2021 Market Data Retrieval.
5. "Teachers' Use of Technology for School and Homework Assignments: 2018–19," NCES, May 2020.
6. Over the last five years, states have shown flexibility with this requirement, especially in the number of programs being approved for adoption.

5

KEEPING THE CUSTOMER SATISFIED

> The release of atomic energy has not created a new problem. It has merely made more urgent the necessity of solving an existing one.
>
> —**Albert Einstein**

When I started at Britannica in 2002, we were still updating and maintaining our legacy print products and developing new ones while we were aggressively investing resources in our e-book product line and reference and learner's websites. But from the downward slope in the sales of our print products that began at the turn of the century and continued through the mid aughts, we knew that we would "eventually" have to go entirely digital, though we did not know exactly when we would make a complete break; print was still bringing in most of the revenue, but margins were shrinking while digital margins were growing.

We had already developed a suite of websites, either from the ground up or by converting content from our print formats, to appeal to our different market segments: Higher education; K-12; library/reference; and consumer, both children and adult. We were encouraged by the sales growth of our

DOI: 10.4324/9781003162636-6

websites, but the level of sales was not yet robust enough to cease selling print altogether. The strategy was only to create print products that we could eventually repurpose for our websites and aim our digital product development at specific segments of the consumer and education markets, and particularly classroom products at all levels, which was the fastest growing of our market segments.

As there was some commonality in the general content of our various websites, with features designed to address the specific requirements of a particular market, I felt that we needed to help our customers in each of our target markets understand our product differentiation better by establishing a separate marketing effort and brand that would service the education segment. So that it would be clear that we had products that were developed exclusively for the classroom or library, I established a division called "Britannica Digital Learning," which then became the global umbrella marketing group for all our K-16 classroom and library products. As a result, we had two clear development and marketing paths, each dedicated to a specific market segment: A consumer division and an education division. Each division had responsibility for developing, pricing, and marketing products according to the needs and expectations of its respective market. The consumer division, which targeted individuals, used two revenue models: Free with advertising support and by subscription. In the education division, all digital products—online databases, curriculum websites, and e-books—were sold by subscription only, with some variation in pricing models between the library and academic market.

In 2012, we famously sold our last print set of encyclopedias, and by this time had stopped selling any print products.[1] Our focus was entirely on our digital offerings and ensuring that we were meeting the needs of our customers and delivering on our value propositions for each of our markets.

Churn low, retain high

Selling digital products, particularly websites, into the library and education market requires knowledge of the demographics of the districts, their curriculum needs, and their budgets. Our sales representatives engaged in consultative selling by first understanding the customer's needs and capabilities and aligning products and services to those needs. To help customers bolster their budgets, we encouraged our reps to learn which federal grants our products qualified for that the districts could use to pay for our products.

If publishers can demonstrate that their products meet a district's curriculum or general content requirements, the district's first step in making a final determination may be to request a trial or agree to conduct a pilot before proposing the product for budget consideration. Of course, there is the caveat that the district can accommodate the technical specifications necessary to implement the product, and if they do, that the publisher, in turn, can meet the district's mandatory requirements, like being able to integrate with their LMS (if they have one) or meet compliance issues around privacy and safety.

Sales cycles for getting any EdTech product into a school, district, or state tend to be long, requiring the involvement and approval of a committee of stakeholders. But once a customer has adopted a product and has fully implemented it across its user base, the publisher's job has just begun; next comes the process of taking the necessary steps to ensure success. The publisher's goal is to earn a customer's loyalty for life, not for a year. To be successful, a publisher must have customers who renew their contracts for multiple years and keep customer churn at a minimum. A successful EdTech product will have an average customer lifetime value (CLTV) of at least five years.

Usage is the currency for customer retention. The more time customers spend on the product, the more likely it is that they will renew. For classroom products, the average renewal rate should be at least 80% less than that indicates something is wrong. Library reference products normally have higher annual renewal rates—close to 100%; once a publisher gets an online reference product into a library budget, the renewal is almost automatic. Every year a new contingent of students matriculates, so the online product is always new to them. However, keeping a customer forever is not realistic. Eventually the customer will want to make a change, or a new committee of buyers will have their own favorite products and priorities, so publishers should anticipate having to fill the void of a lost customer or two at some point.

For their subscription product revenue to grow, publishers must add more customers than they lose every year, or put another way, keep their churn rate as low as possible. Just replacing one customer for every one lost is not growth. Opportunities for growth sprints come when new state adoptions come up and a publisher has the potential to add hundreds of new districts to their customer base. However, when considering whether to enter a state adoption competition, publishers must weigh the total value of the adoption against the current revenue from their existing district customers in that state. Since state adoption contracts equate to a lower per-user fee than a typical district contract, sometimes it is better to pass on an adoption if it means less total revenue than the publisher currently gets from the sum of its district customers.

One of the great advantages of launching an online product is the ability to measure success and demonstrate the value to buyers. Accumulating data on user behavior over time is an empirical way to demonstrate whether the product is underperforming. If the growth in usage has been steady, and users are spending increasingly more time on the product during each session, then it is more likely than not that the school or district will most likely continue to renew the product license—assuming the product category remains a line item in their budget. Still, the publisher should be a proactive partner with a school to help drive usage and maintain customer satisfaction. Here is EdTech guru Vicki Smith Bigham on how her company intervened when a client of hers discovered that some of their customers had become discouraged with the performance of their online products:

A leading educational publisher of K-12 print and online resources was seeking a technical expert to improve documentation and processes for its online products. The company reported weak use of subscription-based electronic products and identified a need for improved user documentation—if that indeed was the problem—but mostly to support implementation and renewal of these products.

The key to customer satisfaction with digital products is setting customer expectations early in the sales process and implementing according to those expectations after the sale is made. It is important, on the front-end of product development, to plan for what the customer will need to know and do and to determine how to make it as easy as possible for the customer to get set up and comfortable to successfully use the product. For many products sold to schools, the "customer" includes multiple people, which may include but not be limited to the curriculum person, the IT resource, the finance office [collectively, buyers], and the teachers and students. The buyers are rarely the users. Presumably if the users are happy, the buyers will be as well.

It is critical to ponder the usage model from the perspective of all stakeholders. What is their experience with your product and processes? Schools do not want to buy problems—they want to buy solutions. Make it easy for the customer—each customer is a stakeholder.

There is incredible bureaucracy in many schools. While it may not seem fair or logical that your company must do so much hand-holding, successful implementation efforts focus on making things easy for the customer and never considering "it is their fault."

This company had put significant resources into product development and partnering to create a robust set of products. It was armed with strong content but lacked a smooth delivery model. There were many internal processes and protocols between the company and its outside developers but little that made the customer experience easier or, at least, anticipated and understood. The model was inefficient and frustrating to the internal team, the sales reps, and the customers. It was reactive rather than proactive.

My company's mandate was to make recommendations regarding ways to improve or enhance current implementation activities and documentation with the goal of making pre-sales, sales, fulfillment, and implementation a more positive experience for all parties involved.

1. **Support independent sales reps in their natural role.**
   Sales reps need a solid understanding of implementation roles and responsibilities for both the company and the customer but should not be in a position of overburdening the customer with specifics of system requirements and implementation needs. The sales rep's role is to get the customer to a qualified point of interest from a curriculum standpoint. Next, the sales cycle must include the implementation discussion, and that point person should be someone other than the sales rep. The implementation

specialist is there to understand and support customer stakeholder roles and can additionally get a sales rep out of a bad or premature sale.

2. **Make the implementation discussion part of the sales cycle but with an implementation specialist.**
Once the customer has interest in purchasing, the implementation specialist should schedule a meeting with *all* identified customer stakeholders necessary for successful implementation. This meeting is calendared and part of the overall sales schedule for every sale to help the customer become aware of and begin to prepare for successful implementation. The meeting should help the customer better understand individual roles and responsibilities with information presented in a manner to ensure that there are no surprises without jeopardizing the sale.

    Create an implementation document to use in this discussion, just as you would any other sales/marketing tool. It should outline expectations, roles, and responsibilities—for the customer and for the company. This mutually agreed-upon document, with contacts in a "chain of escalation," resulting from this meeting, can then be attached to the order form and PO so implementation activities and accompanying contact with the customer begins in positive and expected ways.

3. **As part of implementation, schedule a "checklist" call with the customer prior to activation of the account.**
Once the purchase order has been received, implementation activities begin, but without surprises or having to track down the needed customer contacts and having to explain and/or nag them about what is needed. Schedule a checklist call review to assess progress. Ask specific questions regarding what has been installed and have the customer log in and confirm that the program is working.

    In the strongest models, schools are never left to their own devices. Some companies subcontract installation and configuration and testing work to an outside organization. Others use a per-diem trainer to check and troubleshoot some or all classrooms to better ensure all teachers are set up to easily use the product as intended.

A colleague uses a great metaphor to illustrate what is needed. When you fly into an airport and arrange a shuttle service, you may well have already paid and been told where you will meet the shuttle. But when you arrive and call the service, you are asked several questions. One of those questions is whether you have your luggage. If your response is 'no,' you are not yet ready. Similarly, if the customer has up-front work to do before usage can begin, run through the checklist with them to be sure they are ready.

4. **As part of implementation and once the account has been activated, determine a milestone to again check in with the customer.**
The implementation plan does not end with the first day of anticipated or actual usage. Identify a milestone following activation, e.g., two-three weeks following, for an implementation specialist to follow up with the customer. This may be a time to discuss why there has been no usage and see what kind of support might be helpful. It might be a time to help the customer focus on product capabilities not yet used. The post-launch follow-up contributes to the ongoing nurturing and strengthening of the relationship.

Identifying the cause of the problem—in this case, poor product usage—required an examination of the steps and interactions of all involved from pre-sales through renewal of the product.

Focusing on a process model that effectively communicates roles, responsibilities, expectations, and resources to support implementation early in the sales process decreases the volume of resources needed later to troubleshoot and solve problems and minimizes frustration or negative feelings among internal staff, sales reps, and customers. Realigning resources to reach out to customers at appropriate points, accompanied by relevant and timely documentation, results in a more positive relationship among all parties involved.

Publishers should not have to ask customers how things are going or send them surveys about how often they are using a product or which elements of the product they use the most. By deriving detailed statistics from tracking user behavior with the product, publishers can see the progress in the usage reports. Customers too should be able to access the same reports via a dashboard so that both parties can communicate effectively with the same data in hand. Instead of asking students and teachers whether they like the interface and whether it makes navigation of the product easy, publishers should visit schools so they can watch teachers and students using the product in real time. Observing a user's interaction with a product and gathering data on their usage over time will reveal weaknesses in the user experience and enable publishers to make necessary changes to help maintain customer satisfaction, lower the churn rate, improve retention rates, and increase customer LTV.

Great expectations

Customer expectations for digital products have been and continue to be quite different from what they are for print products. Buyers of physical books clearly understand that their purchase is limited only to what they bought, that nothing about the physical nature of the book in their possession will change over time, and that if they wanted the second or revised edition of the title when it came out, they would have to buy it. This seems obvious and perhaps hardly worth mentioning. But with the advent of digital books, different expectations arose, especially among institutional buyers, who assumed that as changes were made to the content of a title, they would have access to the revised editions as part of their original purchase. In other words, in exchange for not having a physical copy of the book, they thought that a perpetual license to an e-book title included all its revision cycles. I had customers who would assume that when a "new edition" of an e-book title came out, they would be able to access the new edition for free. They felt that the new edition was simply an extension of the same book that they had purchased. This was particularly the case with institutional customers when we published collections of e-book titles that were not available in print. It took time to convince customers that e-books were just books with benefits.

Over time, this sense of entitlement with e-books has evolved; most people understand that an e-book is another format—like hardback, paperback, and audio—and that the title and format they purchased is the edition they will have for the duration of the license. For some time, e-books carried the burden of being part of the digital ecosystem, where changes can be made quickly and seamlessly. Some consumers were under the false assumption that revisions and updates can be made at little or no cost, and that they should be entitled to those revisions with the original purchase. Even though revisions do not require another "edition," as in a print version, they take time and resources to make. Those costs need to be passed on to the consumer.

Today, consumers have much higher expectations for content that they access through subscription websites than they do for e-books or e-zines, and publishers have been complicit in raising those expectations. Customers expect their online subscription content to always be up to date, accurate, fast-loading, responsive on all devices, and constantly changing, improving, and expanding. In theory, depending on the nature of the content, websites should change regularly, and sometimes every day if not frequently during the day. When we log in to the "daily" newspaper, we expect to get "today's" newspaper, but we also expect that it will change over the course of the day. The changes should be fluid, seamless, without having to download the equivalent of what used to be the morning, afternoon, evening, and late editions in print. We also expect to have access to all the previous days' final editions, going back as far as the newspaper has been able to go in digitizing its pre-digital editions.

With our monthly or weekly e-zine subscriptions, we rely on the current issues to be accessible on the websites or appear in our apps on schedule, and we expect to retain access to all previous editions since the beginning of our subscription term. And in between the scheduled issues, we also have access to continually added new content online.

The heightened expectations of what digital products should deliver has also changed our relationship with publishers. Because we have higher and more demanding expectations of the services, we also have a closer bond with the providers of the services. The relationship is ongoing and begins with the start of the subscription transaction. We pay an annual fee upfront in exchange for the promise to receive high-quality service 24 hours a day, 7 days a week. That is quite different from purchasing a single book or magazine and walking away with the totality of the commitment, even if we make a new purchase every day. A subscription is much more personal, and the perception is that the relationship is mutual. We also assume that we are getting far more value for our subscription fees than we could have from a "pay-by-the-drink" model. An ongoing mutual commitment between the publisher and customer should translate into greater consumer product loyalty and a longer CLTV for the publisher.

Because the experience that we have with digital content through apps and websites is so different from that of physical books and magazines, the vocabulary that we use to describe how we interact with digital content has changed as well.

The comparisons between the physical and digital may not always be precise, but for the most part how we "interface" with or "access" a website is different from how we read a book. We open a book to begin our reading journey and "log on" to a website. We look up a word or term in a book, but we "search" a website. As communities, we are readers of books and "users" of websites.

In Table 5.1, I have listed side by side the generally established lexicon we use in each format. This is not meant to be definitive or exact, nor is it meant to place more value on one over the other—but it underscores the qualitative differences in how we generally experience both formats. As my Danish friend, author, and futurist Lene Rachel Andersen puts it, once we have a word for it, we can address it. Words help us understand identity, and the path forward.

Publishing in general will continue to evolve in the direction of EdTech as more outputs are developed first in a digital format and not only by converting print products into websites or apps. The building blocks of Web

Table 5.1 Publishing and EdTech Lexicon

Publishing	EdTech
Readers	Users
Read	Access; read
Layout	Graphical User Interface (GUI)
Open	Log on/log in
Table of contents	Navigation bar
Look up	Search
Scan page	Scroll site
Edition	Current; up to date
Interest level	Engagement
Print; publish	Launch; go live; release; update
Distribute	Implement
Library	Media center
Shelve; archive	Save; store

or app development are not identical to the elements that comprise print. Although some overlap exists between the two, creating and assembling the technology components of a Web product require their own workflow, additional skill sets, and a different business model that considers the cost of, for example, programming and hosting. The more technology-dependent a publisher's product line becomes, the more likely that software engineering will become a core competency.

Whether brought in-house or managed partially as an outsourced adjunct development function, software engineering and design have become such vital activities under a publishers' auspices, and such a large part of their budgets that they have become identified as technology companies as much as they are publishers.

Technology has not only transformed the development of product design and functionality, but by creating product for the Web, publishers own the equivalent of the manufacturing process. With print products, publishers have always partnered with printers to handle the manufacturing; with digital content, publishers are in essence their own manufacturers and own the output stage in the development process. Educational publishers who only publish websites and digital content, and no longer or never did manufacture print products, identify themselves as part of the EdTech industry rather than the publishing industry. The label is not significant, but it moves website publishing from pure product development to the service sector, and like other software companies, to a software as a service (SaaS) business model, which changes the dynamic between product/service provider and customer and raises customer expectations.

As service providers, publishers have acquired talent with new skill sets and developed additional core competencies. Quality assurance, tech support, technical training, technical documentation, statistical reporting, database management, customer support, and retention management are now routine functions within publishing houses with substantial digital products. These functions also transform the company culture, which must make a commitment to customer satisfaction and maintain a relationship with the customer well after the launch of a product. At the same time, when a culture is customer-centric, and customer satisfaction is made a priority, publishers gain more knowledge about their customers' needs and are in a much better position to create products that meet and exceed customers' expectations.

With more direct feedback and data to work with, publishers can customize their websites accordingly and appeal to a broader range of customers, and not only produce products that fulfil the unique requirements of different regions of the country but international markets as well.

Over here, over there

Unless they belong to a large multinational publishing group, or have earned the reputation as a global brand, most American publishers obtain a relatively small part of their total revenue from international sales and licensing. However, most international revenue should derive from the same product developed for the domestic market, and in many cases without having to make major changes. This means that the margins on international revenue represent a significant contribution to the product's ROI. Product development costs are amortized on domestic sales, making international revenue mostly incremental. But even when some adaption is needed to align with another market's commercial requirements, if the products have been produced in a digital format, adaptations and even translations can be made at a fraction of the cost of the original development with much shorter turnaround times.

Digital products can be tested for viability in other markets inexpensively since there is no need to print prototypes or assume the expense of distributing physical samples. In a successful test, a publisher may discover how much or little change is required to provide foreign markets with products that fill a gap in the market and offer a unique value proposition. At a digital conference held in conjunction with the 2017 Shanghai Book Fair, where I participated in a panel discussion on the growth of digital publishing worldwide, the commercial head of Springer Nature in China, an English-German academic publisher part of the Holtzbrinck Publishing Group—and number seven in the list of the top ten largest multinational publishers[2]—told me that they had an annual revenue of over $100 million in China, all with exactly the same digital product line that they publish for the English-speaking market. Except for the sales and marketing costs, Springer was able to leverage their original investment in product development without incurring additional editorial or production costs and successfully find a new, financially significant market opportunity. I would speculate that Springer Nature has had similar success with the same product line in other developed, non-English-speaking countries. Multinationals are an exception in terms of the amount of revenue that they earn from international markets, but the model can be duplicated by any publisher regardless of size.

The opportunity to move efficiently into an international market with an existing English-language product line would not be possible if the product line were not entirely digital. I was told that Springer Nature was not 100% digital with all their products at the time of the Shanghai conference, but they realized from their experience in China, and other markets, the value of doing so as quickly as possible. Their strategic plan called for being all-digital in three years.

Even if a new market requires some product adaptation to be viable, being digital makes it practical and financially feasible to make essential customizations. The resources needed to fulfill the requirements of a new market are far less onerous if the starting point is digital rather than print. At times, publishers need to be reminded of the opportunities that digital content affords and not get hindered by outwardly seeming obstacles. When I was at Britannica I developed, with an outside partner, a photo and image website for the education market called *ImageQuest*, which contained more than 3 million photos and illustrations at launch and grew to over 6 million. With the accompanying metadata, the images were easy to find using a variety of built-in search strategies, including cross-references, related keywords, and captions. *ImageQuest* was offered as a subscription service to schools, libraries, and publishers. Users could access the images for research purposes and download them for any educational, noncommercial project.

ImageQuest became popular with schools and libraries quickly because it offered several benefits over finding and downloading images from the Internet, which students and educators often did. All of the images were: Curated and safe for educational use (no depictions of violence, nudity, and so on); acquired from more than 50 trusted sources like National Geographic, Getty Images, the National Portrait Gallery (London), Bridgeman Images, the Royal Geographical Society, and Newscom; contained full credit and citation information; rendered at the same quality resolution (a standard 150 dpi and 800 pixels on the longest side); and rights-cleared for educational use, which gave institutional heads peace of mind knowing that neither teachers nor students would be inadvertently violating anyone's copyright.

The images depicted people, places, and things from all over the world and on a variety of subjects, and therefore, in theory, could be used by any educational institution in any country that wanted to provide its teachers and students with curated images that came with proper licensing rights, were all the same high quality, and contained no viruses or harmful hidden code, mitigating the risk that students and teachers take every day by downloading random images found on the Internet.

Soon after we launched *ImageQuest*, we had early interest from partners in Brazil, France, Latin America, Egypt, and Japan to create versions of the product in their languages. However, with millions of images—and additional image collections added monthly—continual updating, and the enormous amount of accompanying metadata, translating the entire database into other languages would not have been practical; the effort to do so would have never paid off. As a result, we designed the product in such a way—using a flexible code structure—to allow the user interface to be easily translated and converted into any language. Compared with translating the entire dynamic database, customizing, translating, and adapting only the interface required a minimal effort and cost. We rendered the metadata associated with the images into the target languages by using an automated Google translation tool. This did not result in a perfect translation, but it offered a practical way for speakers of other languages to find and use the photos and other images, which was the main intent of the product; the photos spoke for themselves.

This strategy came in handy when a partner of ours in Wales proposed *ImageQuest* as part of a multiproduct offering in a government tender for primary and secondary schools across the country. Our partner was a local Web developer and content aggregator who had customized their proprietary learning management system (LMS) for the Welsh school system. We both assumed that *ImageQuest* would be perfectly acceptable to the government without any adaptation as Wales is an English-speaking country in the United Kingdom. However, as the Welsh government is proud of its identity and other official language, they insisted that the product be accessible in Welsh. They were happy to include the product as part of the tender, but only if we agreed to make a Welsh-language version available along with the original English. By translating the interface only into Welsh, we satisfied its official language requirement and, at the same time, gave users a choice between English and Welsh with a minimum investment of time and resources. While I was with Britannica, we "translated" *ImageQuest* in this same way into six other languages—Spanish, French, Portuguese, Japanese, Arabic, and Chinese.³

Potential global partners will consider products that have been tested in the first market and have experienced success. Having launched the first foreign-language version of *ImageQuest* made getting other languages on board easier. Brand and reputation can make a difference as well, particularly in some countries, like China, but a brand is less significant than success.

If a publisher has a successful product that garners international interest, equally as important as being able to transfer files with ease is having the worldwide rights to do so. Digital products will invariably contain a variety of media assets—texts, images, video, audio, animations—all of which need to be cleared for worldwide digital use with the copyright holders if they differ from the publisher. To take advantage of any opportunity that may arise in another market, clearing rights may go beyond identifying print or digital formats, but may include audio, Braille, broadcast, and podcast rights as well as compilations like anthologies; even marketing rights may need to be specifically addressed. Peggy Intrator, now Principal of Intrator Associates International Publishing Consultancy, led international rights for one of the multinational educational publishing companies; she tells the following story about rights management:

> I was working in the International Division of a U.S. Educational publisher. We were not creating educational materials specifically for global markets, but if a product was appropriate, we wanted to also be able to sell it in the overseas education market. The challenge was that these programs were often popular because they included many original trade books, mostly by internationally acclaimed authors, and not merely readers written particularly for the program. We knew that we couldn't sell the program if we didn't have rights to sell the trade books outside the United States, so we needed to recontact the original publisher to get first choice, World Rights, and if that wasn't possible, at least Open Market (OM) rights. (For those unfamiliar with licensing terms, when rights have been granted exclusively in North America and the Commonwealth, the rest of the world is typically considered an open market. This

means both the U.S. and the British publisher may sell there. The Open Market excludes any country that is or was once part of the Commonwealth, e.g., Belize, Jamaica, South Africa, Malaysia, and Hong Kong. Sometimes the original publisher or agent sold the British rights to a U.K. publisher, so while the U.S. publisher could give the go-ahead for the rest of the world, some exclusions may have to be separately negotiated.)

Obtaining World or OM rights to include a trade book in an education program, particularly after the program has been published for the United States, presents a real challenge that I'm quite sure was not intended by the original publisher. We were willing to pay to get the rights extended to World/Education Market, which was normally fine with the publisher; the challenge was getting the usually busy rights person to pay attention to what in the end is a financially small request in the scheme of things. It sometimes also involved getting in touch with both the original U.S. publisher as well as the U.K. publisher. Resolving these issues was not rocket science, rather it required tenacity and patience, and, more importantly, it illustrated yet again the importance of personal connections in publishing.

Maintaining intellectual property rights, as well as having completed the technical work necessary to transfer digital content components easily, are the minimum requirements necessary for taking advantage of international opportunities as they develop and extending the value of the initial investments made in product development and marketing. We do, however, live in a political world and issues surrounding government restrictions and censorship that are outside the control of the business community sometimes impede our ability to partner in some countries at certain times.

I have had this come up recently with a partner in China with whom we had a wonderful working relationship that had begun ten years ago and was progressing smoothly and transparently up until the Covid-19 pandemic disrupted world commerce and travel. Even though there were no specific embargoes from the Chinese authorities on continuing to work together, the political atmosphere alone caused our partner to retreat and basically cease communication. The forward momentum and goodwill that had been nurtured over a decade was brough to a halt more by perception than pressure or necessity.

While digital technology and the Internet has made connections between countries easier than ever, and a boon to intercultural exchange, some countries—and for good reasons—have been contemplating the possibility of creating firewalls to block threatening, bellicose, or pornographic content from coming into their cyberspace from outside their borders, turning the Internet into a "splinternet," with virtual boundaries around countries or regions. There may come a time, in fact, when the World Wide Web is not so wide, and the world not so big. Although we may not be able to prevent the disruption caused by a pandemic, we need to thwart bad actors from disrupting global communication and the fluid transference of knowledge that has been nearly 600 years in the making.

Notes

1. The one exception was the annual *Book of the Year*, which continued to be produced until Britannica's 250-year anniversary in 2016.
2. The top ten largest book publishers worldwide in order from top ($5.64 billion) to bottom (1.63 billion) are: RELX Group (UK/NL/US); Thomson Reuters (US); Pearson (UK); Bertelsmann (German); Wolters Kluwer (NL); Hachette Livre (France); Springer Nature (Germany); Wiley (US); HarperCollins (US); and Scholastic (US). From *Statista*, August 2020.
3. A version of the *ImageQuest* anecdote appears in my book *Dealing with Disruption*.

6

FIRST, IDENTIFY THE PROBLEM

> We cannot solve our problems with the same thinking we used when we created them.
>
> —**Albert Einstein**

Most people are probably familiar with the television show *Shark Tank*—which first aired in 2009—where a cast of billionaire and multimillionaire entrepreneurs listen to product pitches from would-be entrepreneurs seeking an investment in exchange for equity in their fledgling companies.[1] The show has resonated so well over 12 seasons for several reasons: The drama around hopeful innovators who strive, and succeed, at getting successful businessmen and women to invest in them and their product concepts and dreams, while others are not so lucky and usually for seemingly good reasons. The show appears to reward a meritocracy, where the good ideas rise, and the bad ones fail. But there is a common denominator to the winners; when the "sharks" explain why they decided to buy into a pitch and invest in the product and inventor, the reason is almost always because the product appears to solve a real problem in a unique way, and the inventor

DOI: 10.4324/9781003162636-7

is not only passionate but appears trustworthy. Regardless of their style and how they evaluate the products and the inventors, the sharks reward products that solve common, everyday problems and have the potential to earn customer loyalty by demonstrating a more efficient, convenient solution. Likewise, over the years we have seen innovative publishers, especially in EdTech, leverage digital technology to solve problems and improve consumer experiences with knowledge-based products. Some of the solutions may have been expressly applied to their customer base or their own company's infrastructure, while others have changed the way many of us consume information and knowledge.

Throughout the chapters in this book, I have recounted anecdotes from my publishing colleagues that exemplify how digital technology has transformed the publishing industry, necessitated new business models, and altered our relationship to information and knowledge. In soliciting their contributions, I asked them to share a problem that they had resolved that made a meaningful impact on their internal organization, clients, or customers. The narratives they provided varied depending on their role. The CEOs or senior executives acting as "intrapreneurs" solved problems that improved the workflow in their organizations or their customers' experiences with their products or services; the consultants described problems that were brought to them from their clients; and the entrepreneurs acquired loyal customers by solving an industry problem or myriad problems in a unique way. What they all had in common was how they used digital technology to find solutions that were scalable and could be used repeatedly to get similar results. Some solutions were unique to a specific problem and situation, but others could be universally applied—just as we have seen Zoom or Google Meet enable most of K-12 and higher education institutions switch seamlessly to remote learning during the pandemic.

In almost every industry since March of 2020, the pandemic has certainly been the mother of many inventions. At the same time, digital technology has made it possible to solve problems in publishing that arose long before the pandemic and have helped us pivot to remote learning when we needed to.

In the late 1990s, forward thinking product developers used content-rich databases to perform tasks that today we assign to desktop-publishing software. Vicki Bigham, who led an innovative educational consulting firm for more than 30 years, describes how she and her partner helped a client produce a print directory with metadata created from the client's source material:

Our company had a contract with a major educational publisher of print and digital content for the middle school through high school and higher education markets to produce a directory of online education resources. The directory identified websites of particular importance to K-12 educators, parents, and students and was published as a printed book with an accompanying CD-ROM, as those were the predominant formats being used in schools at the time.

It was 1997, before the heavy dependence on the Internet, but a *book* about websites still seemed like an anomaly. Because my business partner, and husband, was a database developer, we proposed creating the body of the manuscript with the FileMaker Pro database to make it easy to update the work and to additionally keep our options open as regards to creating other electronic versions if the client so desired. While an online version or website never occurred to us, we ended up creating a layout in FileMaker that allowed the publisher, for the first time ever, to go straight to print from an author's "manuscript." *(Figure 6.1, Directory Layout 1.)*

That was back in the "FileMaker Pro 5" days, so it was a single flat file, nothing relational about the database. We had 21 fields per record, most of them text. A container field held a single graphic for each website. There were nine layouts, with three important ones:

- Data Entry—The one our team used to enter information about each website.
- New Dir-2—This was the third and final directory layout (*Figure 6.2, Final Directory Layout*), the one the publisher used to print to film directly from FileMaker.
- And Statistics—A layout (and script) that generated a report to let us know progress toward completion, i.e., how many records we had for each subject category and subcategory.

There were set numbers of blank pages at the beginning of the final manuscript and another 11 scattered throughout the file so that the

Site Title	Aesop's Fables Online Exhibit	
Site URL	http://ww.pacificnet.net/johnr/aesop	
Sponsor	John R. Long, STAR SYSTEMS	
Subject Area	Language Arts	Nominated By: Kathy Schrock's Guide for Educators
Subcategory	Literature	Grade Level: Elementary, Middle School, High School
Description	Come read and in some cases, hear the fables of Aesop, both those you have heard time and again as well as perhaps some that will be new. The online exhibit includes over 600 fables, some with Real Audio narrations and images, some random fables, and a search engine; more is promised.	
Commentary	"One good turn deserves another." "A man is known by the company he keeps." "An ounce of prevention is worth a pound of cure." As students of Aesop know, each fable has a moral. Lessons abound here, whether you are studying or reading for enjoyment. The site is frequently updated, so return often to hear stories and things to think about from the master storyteller.	
GIF	AESOP'S FABLES [Image Here]	Action Items-VSB
GIF File Name	Aesop2.jpg Date created: Date modified: 7/23/1998	
GIF Status	YES Record Compete? YES VSB Approved? YES	
Site Rejected-Date-By-Reason		
Chapter	01. Curriculum Corner Record Owner LangArts-VSB-12/97	

Figure 6.1 Directory Layout 1.

publisher could make the page numbering come out correctly, using their own front-matter files and between-section pages.

There were several value lists, such as for Grade Level: Preschool, Elementary, Middle School, etc. One script printed the Statistics report and a second sorted records and printed a draft of the directory.

More than two decades later, it is more than likely that many of the URLs listed in the directory no longer exist. But at the time, it was a successful publishing effort that gave the client the product that they needed with the advantage of having a database that could be revised electronically and leveraged to produce other outputs in the future if they wanted to.

In short, having this content in a digital database afforded the publisher options for several derivative products and formats. They could add to the

| "THE OLD MANSE" | Site: 19th Century American Writers
Location: http://www.tiac.net/users/eldred/nh/html
Sponsor: Eric Eldred
Subject Areas: Language Arts   Sub-Category: Literature
Grade Levels: Middle School, High School |

Description
This listing of 19th Century American writers is ordered by birth with links to references about each one. There is a glossary of words, which might be unfamiliar to readers of these works. Since all links are external files, the information varies by author.

Commentary
Different authors seem to be featured from time to time. The logo pictured is from The Old Manse by Nathaniel Hawthorne. There is extensive material about his life and works, including several portraits.

|  | Site: A Literary Index: Internet Resources in Literature
Location: http://www.vanderbilt.edu/english/litIndex.html
Sponsor: Chris Flack
Subject Areas: Language Arts   Sub-category: Literature
Grade Levels: High School |

Description
The Web site offers an overview and a review of collections of Internet literary resources. Contents include Literature Indices; Doing Literary Research; Departments and Literary Institutes; Archives of Electronic Texts, Books, and Presses; Composition, Rhetoric, and Writing; and The Teaching of Literature.

Commentary
There are many excellent resources included here. Teachers will appreciate the Teaching of Literature section, and teachers and students alike will certainly find some resources of particular interest in the Composition, Rhetoric, and Writing section—possibilities include links to Teaching with Excellence, World-Wide-Web resources for Rhetoric and Composition, and others.

| Aesop's Fables | Site: Aesop's Fables Online Exhibit
Location: http://www.pacificnet.net/johnr/aesop
Sponsor: John R. Long, STAR SYSTEMS
Subject Areas: Language Arts   Sub-category: Literature
Grade Levels: Elementary, Middle School, High School |

Description
Come read and, in some cases, hear the fables of Aesop, both those you have heard time and again as well as perhaps some that will be new. The online exhibit includes over 600 fables, some with Real Audio narratives and images, some random fables, and a search engine; more is promised.

Commentary
"One good turn deserves another." "A man is known by the company he keeps." "An ounce of prevention is worth a pound of cure." As students of Aesop know, each fable has a moral. Lessons abound here, whether you are studying or reading for enjoyment. The site is frequently updated, so return often to hear stories and things to think about from the master storyteller.

Figure 6.2 Final Directory Layout.

database over time and continue to print the directory, they could re-issue the CD-ROM or DVD, or they could eventually create a website of URLs. Vicki and her team gave the client options that they had not anticipated and enabled the client to repurpose the content in the future.

Youth communication: amplifying powerful young voices

Established in 1980 in New York City, Youth Communication (YC) is a non-profit organization that publishes powerful, teen-written stories and provides professional development curriculum and training to help educators and youth workers engage and motivate young people. Their literacy-rich training model helps teachers, counselors, and other professionals connect with teens and their priorities and build their social and emotional learning skills. Youth Communication is the only organization dedicated exclusively to publishing authentic stories by middle- and high-school students.

Prior to the pandemic, besides having an organizational marketing website, Youth Communication had not yet entered the digital age. They published periodic print magazines and newspapers, which they would send to schools and organizations that had been on their mailing list for several decades. These publications were delivered free of charge and paid for by donations to the organization. Their audience tended to be localized around the New York City area where all the student writers resided.

The organization never intended to commercialize the students' publishing efforts, though they did work with other publishers to license and sell their professional development curriculum products and services. But their focus has been and is the student writings, to provide a platform for young authors and to share their personal stories—to make a difference in their lives and the lives of their readers.

With limited resources and a history of publishing only in print, it was difficult for YC to have an impact beyond a small geographical area. They would never be able to print and distribute enough copies to make anywhere near the impact that they could make if they published their content online so that anyone with Internet access could gain access to their stories. By going digital, not only would they have a national impact, as their board had encouraged them to do, but they could reach an international audience as well.

YC board member, Bill Smith, oral historian and publisher at BiographyPARTNER, provides context on how YC came to the decision to change the way that they had been publishing for more than 40 years:

Since 1980, New York City's Youth Communication (YC) has helped at-risk high school students tell their stories. Our writers have experienced foster care, homelessness, juvenile justice, and hail from New York City's most distressed neighborhoods. Ninety percent are teens of color. Their stories describe the challenges they face and the social and emotional skills they use to overcome them. YC stories are the foundation for our acclaimed social and emotional learning (SEL) curriculum and professional development used by educators across the country.

YC has won virtually every award in educational publishing. Alumni writers include MacArthur Genius, Edwidge Danticat; journalist, Veronica Chambers; Michelle Obama biographer and journalist, Rachel Swarns; Founder and CEO of the Campaign for Black Male Achievement, Shawn Dove; and hundreds of others who have gone on to serve as educators, activists, and advocates for a new generation.

On Thursday, March 12, 2020, Betsy Cohen—barely three months into her new job as Youth Communication Executive Director—gathered her staff to confront the impending shutdown of New York City schools, the survival of the organization, and most importantly, getting help to the stricken middle- and high-school students hit hard by the pandemic.

Youth Communication: Live from Covid-19 New York
Lessons from the pandemic

Betsy Cohen, Executive Director of Youth Communication

Setting an end goal

I started as Executive Director ten weeks before the crisis. I thought I was stepping in to grow an SEL [social and emotional learning] program built on a legacy of print magazines and an archive of

9,000 stories with a clunky digital strategy. My priority was scaling SEL curriculum and training based on in-person work and in-print curriculum. That is what the market wanted and what we planned to continue to build.

In March of 2020, the entire country was suddenly looking at New York. New York was the focal point of the pandemic. I began to get frantic communications from funders, from board members, and peers that YC had to quickly focus on planning for the worst-case scenario. The virus was coming, and it was coming fast.

I remember everything moved so quickly. I felt an enormous need to act and act now. It was especially important to me not to overreact or to become more afraid. I felt that if we did not act immediately and make ourselves relevant and of service to our community, YC might not survive the crisis.

I knew I had decisions to make that I wasn't equipped to make. I didn't know what I was doing, but I knew that I needed to try to steer this ship to the other side. I told myself to be steady, to look to the positive for my team, and to try to maintain integrity and not compromise my character during this time of panic. My best-self wondered, not just "Will Youth Communication survive? But *If we survive*, where do we want to be when this is over?"

Listening

Right away, one of our writers, a teen commuting from South Brooklyn, had written this thoughtful e-mail about why he was choosing not to come into the office. He said that he was not going to take the subway because he didn't want the responsibility of getting someone else sick. When you have a 15-year-old showing you that what you must worry about is not, "How are you going to be okay?" but, "How are you going to be a part of caring for others?" you can't help but listen.

So, on that Thursday when staff confronted what to do if we could not come back to work on Monday, we immediately asked, "What can we learn from the kids?"

One of the editors said, "Our kids are feeling really afraid. What's going to happen to them when this gets really bad?" Our writers have always been the so-called "canary in the coal mine" for us. My colleague Tim said, "If our kids are afraid, kids everywhere are afraid." Tim said, "What can we do for them? If it's not going to be business as usual—training, curriculum, and predictable teachers in front of the class—then how can we help our community?"

At that moment, it clicked that our Covid-19 mission was to go back to our roots. Youth Communication needed to figure out how to amplify the voices of young people. During a crisis, we always have the most to learn from people on the margins. Marginalized people suffer the most when the system is ripped apart. YC was founded because we understood that young people are always on the cutting edge of social justice and progressive ideals. These are voices that most people never get to hear. To read the deep, thoughtful, *felt* reflections of these urban teens made it impossible not to feel the pandemic.

One of our kids had a brother who was working at a grocery store and got sick. Then his whole family got sick. He wrote a story about the feelings of his entire family being affected. The story was about their fear and about the systemic economic inequalities present for his family.

We published a story from a teenage mother living with her young child in foster care. She wrote about how—after she had gotten all these social services and options lined up: School, counselling, a nurse to help with the baby, all these things she had set up to manage her life—they immediately fell away with the virus.

One sweet 15-year-old wrote about how she had been preparing for her dance recital all year. It was a big deal in terms of her confidence and sense of accomplishment and the feelings of disappointment when it got pulled out from under her. Leila's story about her dance recital was not the biggest loss by any means, but it was typical of what kids were going through and the kind of universal human story that people needed to hear. To be a megaphone for young voices is a huge part of what YC is here to do.

Being adaptive

At first, the situation was not at all clear. One scenario was that schools would reopen before the end of the year. But, by mid-April, it was obvious we weren't going back. Graduations were canceled, proms were canceled, and people were wondering what happens with college in the fall? How do you keep a second-semester senior engaged and caring about graduation when everything they've worked for is being pulled out from under them? The situation was changing every day, everyone was feeling loss, fear, and confusion about the future.

There was a gift in facing the chaos as a new executive director. Being new allowed for a lack of rigidity or preciousness about having to let go. Part of any leadership is questioning the value and processes of what came before. I was open to what YC might do better and I had an advantage in being adaptive and questioning what a longer-term leader might have taken for granted.

Which isn't to say that I didn't panic about what we might be losing. YC had just completed a strategic planning process. I felt a deep concern about not being able to fulfill a plan that so many stakeholders had invested in so many ways. "Was our planning wasted?" That was hard for me. But as we moved forward, that planning provided YC with a clear vision of what we did that was essential and important and the role we had to play in "Covid-19 New York City."

Connecting

I was listening and learning from everyone around me. I began having conversations with other executive directors, funders, board members, and staff. Everyone was working together with full generosity to manage the impact of Covid-19. Every group that I was a part of became an important lifeline. There was so much eagerness for connection. March–April 2020 presented a unique opportunity to connect because folks were all talking about the same thing. We were all just trying to stay afloat. Everyone's life had been upended. In the spring of 2020, no one was having a normal day.

That community experience was unlike anything I've ever experienced. I am a person who really values relationships and networking: Being there for others and calling upon others when I need support. Every time you reached for a life raft, you were providing a life raft for someone else. There was a tremendous balance of giving.

I talked to a friend who worked for a big research organization. She has a broad view of what other programs were struggling with and she is very committed to racial justice. My friend said, "People are watching who's struggling right now. People are watching New York. Youth Communication has the voices of young people, something no one else has. Everybody wants to hear those voices now. Go share their stories."

That really shifted my thinking, "This wasn't a moment to stick to the norm; this was a moment to get out there and provide what was essential." Nobody else had our stories. People are moved by personal stories and it was essential—in any context—that we get our stories out to the world. That clarity made more nuanced adaptations way more feasible to get behind emotionally.

Essential and important

Another friend was the director of a New York Community school. I asked, "What do your teachers need right now?" His answer was, "Whatever you do, make it standards aligned."

School districts were reporting student trauma and anxiety at an all-time high. The need for SEL materials had skyrocketed. But, in a crisis, SEL skills are not core academic concepts that a teacher checks off the list.

All our conversations were that teachers were struggling with connecting with their kids. Teachers were overwhelmed and needed to triage just to provide the absolute academic essentials. Every day, teachers were reinventing the wheel figuring out how they were even going to get online; getting kids computers, trying to get them logged in. The need for us to respond fast felt so important. There was no time to be overly thoughtful, it was just, "Let's figure out what we can do and get our best out there." Within weeks, we had developed standard-based remote English Language Arts lessons for our stories.

YC rapidly shifted to providing all services remotely. We began to provide remote coaching and editing to our teen writers. We launched *Inside Voices*, a free biweekly online newsletter, distributed to 9,000 educators and community members who were now able to hear from teens they might not otherwise learn from.

In lieu of our expected professional development, we created free bi-weekly online workshops for teachers. On April 2, we hosted our first webinar. We teamed with New York's *Student Success Network* and Dave Adams from Urban Assembly to discuss, *"How to foster SEL growth with Remote Learning."*

Registration happened fast. Within days, 800 educators signed on—eight times our normal attendance, including educators from across the world. The power of our stories inspired conversations between hundreds of people sharing how they were connecting with their kids. It was a beautiful kind of catharsis, an exhale moment for these devoted people to say, "Here's how I'm showing up for my kids."

Resources were needed, but I think human connection was also really needed. After you've heard the story of a young person's fear and anxiety, it may feel a little more normal to bare your own soul to 100 strangers on a Zoom call. Over the next couple of months, we led five webinars that reached over 2,100 people internationally, mostly teachers and counselors in SEL from the United Kingdom, Australia, and Canada.

In late May, when George Floyd was killed, it only got more complex. Now everybody was thinking about our police in New York City and racial justice across the country. Youth voices, and particularly the marginalized voices of youth of color, were the dramatic starting point of an important change in the power dynamics of institutions combatting white supremacism. We were all dealing with this collective trauma. Once again, YC kids led us through with their stories. Processing emotions is an instructional tool, but it's also a powerful human tool.

YC's Covid-19 stories of March and April were powerful for that moment. The racial justice stories of the summer and even more recently are reflective of our ongoing struggle and will hopefully be valuable for years to come.

The new normal

Now, I reflect about the new normal, what has changed, and what our world will look like if/when we come through this. There are so many questions particularly about race and capitalism that may have shifted forever.

There are physical changes in New York City, in our country, and in our world. We are all feeling anxious. Everyone is feeling disconnected. There is new awareness of social emotional well-being. People everywhere, and in an incredibly special way—educators— are coming forward with a changed understanding of their primary role in undoing racism. By centralizing the voices of young people, YC is in a unique position to help.

The pandemic created an opening and I'm excited about it. I want to be ready. I look back on what we accomplished by listening, connecting, and focusing on what this organization has that is essential and important. We have the voices of youth, voices that need to be heard. "Where do I want Youth Communication to be when this is over? I want this organization and these stories to be everywhere."

Once Betsy made the decision to publish in a digital publishing environment, she made it possible to achieve the organization's goals. When I talked to her last, she told me that they were currently mentoring 45 youth writers, had published 100 previously written stories on their website, posted stories on social media to drive traffic to their website, and were creating a variety of e-zines. They were publishing a 1,200- to 1,500- word story each week. All of their content was distributed "open access" to extend their reach, build their brand, and stimulate interest in YC and their professional development programs. By all accounts, success came early. They had already secured contracts with several educational publishers to incorporate their stories into the publishers' Language Arts programs.

Betsy says they have no intention of returning to print unless it is with a licensing partner. If someone else wants to license their content for a print product, they would be happy to accommodate that request. They anticipate producing podcasts in the future as well, expanding their social media presence, and possibly creating marketing pieces that will create more awareness around their activities. In the meantime, their professional education initiatives are getting more popular, especially their digital curriculum lessons for teachers that include 18 stories per lesson from their high-school student writers. The materials have all been adapted for virtual presentations over video chat platforms like Zoom or Google Meet.

Open sesame

With a free Internet and open access to most websites, it was inevitable that an effort would be made to put some structure and guidelines around the use of freely available content. Government organizations, non-profits, public institutions, as well as many scholars, educators, and freelance journalists were eager to make their content open to the public without permissions or fees to fulfill their missions, give back to their community, gain recognition and trust, and reach as large an audience as possible. But some usage parameters needed to be established to protect copyrights and content ownership and to ensure that other entities or individuals could not take credit for work that was not theirs or use it for their own benefit and financial gain.

In 2001, the non-profit organization Creative Commons (CC) was founded to make educational and creative work freely available with the stipulation that it could not be used for commercial purposes. Another objective of CC was to avoid wrapping unnecessary red tape around the use of content for non-commercial purposes. If the new work would not be monetized in any way—online or offline—the author of that work would not have to obtain permission to use the original content. Through designated licenses on CC, the authors of original works determine which rights they reserve, and which rights they are willing to waive, in lieu of the "All rights reserved" language in standard copyright law. These licenses allow the free use of CC content, primarily text and photos, for all non-commercial purposes.

The massive *Wikipedia* project, for example, which is a free site void of advertising, has a Creative Commons license. Based on its popularity as one of the top ten most visited websites, *Wikipedia* could be earning hundreds of millions of dollars per year if it were able to accept advertising revenue.[2] But it cannot, nor can it have a paywall of any kind because it is populated with User Generated Content (UGC)—volunteers from around the world contribute articles and edits to the site without compensation. Although the Wikipedia foundation accepts donations, if they were to receive revenue from the *Wikipedia* site, they would have to share it with the contributors, which would be a nearly impossible feat given the thousands of worldwide contributors and their anonymity. The foundation is stuck with their model; they cannot put the genie back in the bottle.

OER (Open Educational Resources) Commons was founded a year after the Creative Commons by the non-profit Institute for the Study of Knowledge Management in Education (ISKME) with a mission "to improve the practice of continuous learning, collaboration, and change in the education sector. . . ISKME conducts social science research, develops research-based innovations, and facilitates innovation that improves knowledge sharing in education."[3] OER Commons has become the largest repository of curriculum materials in the English language—submitted by individual educators, writers, and specialists—that can be used as a resource by teachers and curriculum developers to collaborate on pedagogical best practices and generate additional materials. With a grant from the William and Flora Hewlett Foundation in 2007, OER Commons was able to create a digital library of free materials that are curated, peer-reviewed, aligned to standards, and shared freely under Creative Commons licenses. The process that the curriculum materials go through to be included in the digital library makes the resources trusted and highly desirable to the education community.

Amit Shah, Founder and Managing Director of Green Comma, an educational service provider, has been an OER advocate since the early days in the formation of the Creative Commons and OER Commons. He describes how he has relied on both organizations to create content for a major K-12 publisher:

Open Education Resources (OER) was only a glimmer on the publishing horizon about 15 years ago. I was working with one of

the top four K-12 publishing companies at that time and there was a constant search online to see how instructors across the nation were creating their own courses utilizing online materials that the publisher provided for classroom use as part of the paid instructional set of materials. These customizations were illegal and sometimes were shut down by applying the legal arm of the publishers. Often, though, they were simply given a pass by the publisher so as not to muddy the goodwill of the district and risk losing a customer.

What these customizations demonstrated to me was the need for instructors to incorporate online materials in their personal collection, "own" them, so to speak, and give minimal credit without paying exorbitant fees. OER Commons provided the thrust that filled this need and online customized materials took off.

In 2008, I started a curriculum development and publishing services company, Green Comma, and as a marketing tool in 2015 started developing free OER discussion materials, primarily on current events and issues, for use in grades ten and above. The only requirement for use was to give Green Comma credit under the Creative Commons attribution and licensing agreement. Utilizing existing online links, independent author-generated content, and royalty-free images, we have since produced over 25 such discussions, ranging from minimum wage, surveillance and national security, and the value of cryptocurrency, to menstrual hygiene and poverty, and DACA [Deferred Action for Childhood Arrivals].

With Creative Commons licenses and OER, open access content has become a reliable source of curriculum materials and a way to scale development and improve brand awareness, even if the content does not receive the same scrutiny as professionally curated and edited content produced by established publishers. Some have likened the effort to Open-Source Software (OSS) development, where source code is developed collaboratively by volunteer programmers and is free for use by anyone who understands how to implement and maintain it. Although there may be some similarities in the licensing regulations of OSS and OER, the former requires a level of technical expertise, access permissions, and stringent peer review that is not required by the latter. Still, the OER initiatives demonstrate the willingness of thousands of educators and curriculum developers to contribute their experience and ideas, and to allow anyone to use them in accordance with the licensing restrictions without any compensation.

Without implying a direct causal link—since I am not aware of one—another initiative that sprang to life shortly after the creation of OER was the open distribution of MOOCs (Massive Open Online Courses), developed by university professors from the courses they were teaching at their institutions. Early popular MOOCs came out of Stanford in 2011 by Peter Norvig and Sebastien Thrun, who offered their "Introduction to Artificial Intelligence" course to students worldwide. Thrun went on to found Udacity, a company devoted to creating MOOCs and offering them for free, while Andrew Ng and Daphne Koller, also Stanford professors, started Coursera, which partnered with universities to develop and distribute MOOCs at reasonable prices.

MIT and Harvard joined together in the creation of a platform for MOOCs and opened a non-profit consortium called edX, which now claims to have more than 3,000 courses and 160 member universities, as well as dozens of corporations, worldwide.

Most MOOCs are created by professors within their universities and are offered as part of the university's curriculum. The original market for the courses was meant to be internal and financed from student tuition and other university funding sources. By offering the same quality courses that full-time students at premier universities take for free through edX, universities enhance their reputation as educational innovators and thought leaders, which raises their profile and can serve as an indirect recruiting tool for future students, faculty, and grants—basically giving the sleeves out of their vests. Although students who take the MOOCs have no relation to the universities and do not get any credit for taking them, they can advance their knowledge and skills for free.

I have not taken any MOOC courses myself, but I have taken several 12-lesson asynchronous courses from Gale/Cengage offered free through my local library. Each lesson required 2–3 h to complete depending on how much extra practice you invested, amounting to about the equivalent of a one-semester course. I found them to be excellent on delivering on their stated objectives, and they were a productive way to fill extra time during the pandemic. Prior to the pandemic, I had a client that had developed over 200 online courses on careers and electives for middle and high school and community colleges. They too did an effective job of providing engaging content and allowing the students to pace themselves through the material and receive feedback from the teacher when necessary by means of an online discussion area in the course platform. They sold the courses directly to schools through their sales force, but they also licensed them to other publishers as a "white label" platform that the licensee could rebrand and distribute under their own name.

Online courses have their downsides and detractors, not usually because of the content but because of the isolation of the learner working alone on a computer without the ability to engage in real time with fellow learners. For that reason and others, online course may not be the only way to present curriculum, but they solve several problems at once. They enable students to work from any place at any time and to progress at their own pace, without time limits; make curriculum subjects available that the school would not be able to offer any other way; empower students to take control of their learning; utilize multimedia for increased engagement; and through online chat areas, create opportunities for students to interact with their peers regardless of where they live, their backgrounds, and their experiences. Many educators are enthusiastic advocates of hybrid models, where schools supplement traditional in-class teaching and collaboration with online courses.

Notes

1. The U.S.-produced *Shark Tank* is based on the British broadcast *Dragons' Den*, which first aired in 2005 and was loosely based on *Tigers of Money*, which originated in Japan in 2001. Apparently *Shark Tank* more closely resembles *Dragons' Den*, though I have not seen it or its Japanese predecessor.
2. According to Alexa, a Web analytics site, as of March 1, 2021, Wikipedia.org is ranked 7th in the United Kingdom, 8th in the United States, and 13th globally.
3. Taken from the ISKME website, https://www.iskme.org/March 3, 2021.

7

THE MEDIA AND THE MESSAGE

> Condense some daily experience into a glowing symbol, and an audience is electrified.
>
> —**Ralph Waldo Emerson**

The popularity of multimedia in almost all publishing categories has only risen with the increasing number of publications on the Web. Magazines, newspapers, and educational websites make frequent use of videos, animations, audio, 3-D infographics, and podcasts. Media in all formats are being embraced to increase consumer engagement. In early 2021, Amazon, which transformed the way we buy books and provided a platform for self-publishers to easily create, publish, and sell their books, followed Apple and Google Play by offering podcasts in their streaming music service.

Audiobooks have exhibited more growth than any other publishing category. According to a recent article by Deloitte, the audiobook and podcasting markets are growing far faster than the overall media and entertainment markets.[1] Although audiobooks represent only a fraction of the revenue earned by books and newspapers, by some estimates audiobooks

DOI: 10.4324/9781003162636-8

and podcasts will have grown by 25–30% in 2020, while the growth of other media and entertainment sectors hovers at around 4%.

Clearly, audiobooks are on a steep upward curve. The category has succeeded in scratching a general itch: We can listen to books while driving, commuting, and exercising, and catch up on our reading without having to read. For the visually challenged, it is a substitute for reading, especially if many books are not available in other formats that also assist people with visual challenges—like Braille or Daisy (Digital Accessible Information System). Children's audiobooks have grown significantly; in China, this category represented 40% of audiobook sales in 2020. Like any medium, content matters most, and if the content is engaging, by rendering it an audiobook format—with the right voice, background music, and atmospherics—the end result can constitute a compelling, convenient experience, as well as an incremental growth opportunity for publishers.

Tim Ditlow, VP of Content at Epic, a leading e-book website for children and educators, was a pioneer of audiobooks, but not just any audiobooks. Tim's story is one for the ages, and this is the first time that he has told it in a published work:

"Book about a boy wizard getting good reviews." That was the message I received shortly after the 1997 London Book Fair from Kate Walsh, my editorial contact at Chivers Audio in Bath, England, asking me to join them on a bid for the audiobook rights for *Harry Potter and the Philosopher's Stone* by J.K. Rowling.

At the time I was running Listening Library, a family-owned audiobook company in Old Greenwich, Connecticut, and I had a co-production venture with Chivers, where we scouted the best children's books on both sides of the pond looking to acquire audio rights for our respective territories. We then produced the recordings wherever it made most sense, primarily in London and New York City.

Kate's simple note led to a rather fierce auction where I ended up winning the audiobook rights to what became *Harry Potter and the Sorcerer's Stone* here in the United States.

The backstory on the casting of British actor Jim Dale for the project, and the critical and sales success of the entire seven-title audiobook series, has received a fair amount of press over the years. Jim won multiple Grammy awards and he ended up in the Guinness Book of World Records for creating the most character voices for an audiobook. For the better part of 1999–2007, the Harry Potter books and audiobooks were a major force in the children's book world expanding expectations of what children will read or listen to if their interest is piqued.

However, what has not been written about is how challenging it was to bring these audio titles to market. The late 1990s were still the days of cassettes and CDs and digital streaming was just on the horizon. The first three recordings came out in rapid succession as the U.S. market raced to catch up with the earlier release of the print books in Britain where the series originated.

Then a 636-page manuscript marked "HPIV"—aka *The Goblet of Fire*, the fourth volume in the series—was hand delivered to my office by Rowling's U.S. publisher, Scholastic. Our audiobook version was going to be published simultaneously for the first time with both the U.S. and the U.K. print editions on July 8, 2000, and the clock was already ticking. Loudly. A book of that length would be a massive undertaking in every way. And how were we going to create a children's retail box to hold 17 CDs? The previous release, *Harry Potter and the Prisoner of Azkaban*, clocked in at a mere ten CDs.

I immediately called Ken Golden, the president of Tri-Plex Packaging, who had handled all the retail design work for Listening Library going back to the early 1990s. I outlined the challenge and asked him to come and meet with my art director at Random House Audio, Jennifer Lee. (Side note: I had sold Listening Library to Random House in 1999.)

We knew a 17-CD audiobook for children was going to be a difficult endeavor as the weight alone was almost two pounds. This may not be unusual today but at that time the retail market focused mostly on abridgements with four to five CDs being the standard. In addition, the Harry Potter audiobook sales figures were setting new industry records. So, not only were we up against a tight deadline, but the sheer volume of the number of units we would need to manufacture, ship, and collate by hand was daunting. Think of the math on 17 CDs times hundreds of thousands of units! Sonopress, our CD replicator, was accustomed to single CD production based on the music industry so this kind of volume put our numbers on the level of artists like Garth Brooks and Britney Spears who were also on press around that time. Production occurred around the clock to meet the demand.

Ken came in with a mock-up that none of us had seen before. It was a two-piece telescoping box and five CD wallets each capable of holding four CDs. Jennifer immediately saw these wallets as an opportunity to use four-color printing options on both sides, forming a 20-frame mini-canvas that would showcase many of the beautifully designed artwork elements by acclaimed Harry Potter illustrator Mary GrandPré. And when all five wallets were placed in the box, another image of Harry was displayed across the spines. This book was pivotal to the entire Harry Potter series arc, and we all agreed that the packaging had to reflect what was a turning point in the series as Rowling's storytelling became darker.

While this might seem difficult to imagine in the current reality of the Harry Potter franchise, in 2000, there was the book. And the audiobook. There were no films, theme parks, scarves, Quidditch brooms, or Bertie Bott's Beans. Also, it was unusual to have the audio rights to a major bestseller not under the same corporate roof as the hardcover book. Listening Library was working closely with Scholastic's Harry Potter team to help give children another way of understanding and enjoying the vibrant world J.K. Rowling had invented. Who knew centaurs have Welsh accents?

We were inspired not only to deliver the story via Jim Dale's remarkable voice, but to also offer young listeners a physical package that could help them feel part of this wizarding world.

It was a risk to invest this much money on a retail package because we were not sure if a family would be willing to spend $70.00 on a children's audiobook. And we needed to find a design with a compact footprint so that this release could fit into existing store displays and could also stand up on a retail counter. In this case we had to not only come up with the box, but to think both outside and inside the box!

Looking back at what felt like a frenzied time, I now better appreciate how I was able to draw upon contacts made over decades in publishing to connect people who are experts in their field and make this happen. By nurturing these professional relationships, you can confidently face the demands of working in any industry knowing you can rely on the trust you have built. There will always be disruptions or a disruptive project, but what cannot be sidelined is an imaginative and efficient process in your supply chain starting with your creative team.

A few postscripts:

Jennifer Lee, our talented art director, was attending film school at night during those early and hectic Harry Potter years, and I am happy to say that she went on to write and direct *Frozen* and is now the chief creative officer at Walt Disney Animation Studios.

Ken Golden is still running Tri-Plex Packaging and finding new ways to dazzle consumers with his creative approach to showcasing retail products.

As for me, for the past seven years I have been working as the VP, Content, at Epic, the leading digital reading platform for children, helping to build a library of over 45,000 titles.

Video has also been on an ascending trend in all of publishing categories, with a wide variety of applications and production values. The use of video in education, however, has been hampered by accessibility issues, format standards, and institutional budgets. Inconsistent quality in educational video content, especially content written specifically for the curriculum areas, has been another factor in the slow growth of video in the education market despite the heightened interest in making more use of the medium. These were problems waiting for solutions.

By the mid-1980s, the previously standard 16-mm format for educational videos were transferred mostly to VHS or Beta tapes, which required new hardware purchases that many schools could not find a place for in their budgets. When DVDs arrived a decade later, additional hardware barriers presented the same impediments. By the early aughts, several video production companies made DVDs available for download. But this put the burden on schools to figure out how to increase their server capacity—assuming they even had servers—and provide the technology necessary for teachers to use in a class. A tall order at the time, and today as well for many schools.

Andrew Schlessinger, CEO & co-founder of SAFARI Montage, took giant steps forward in finding a more permanent solution for making high-quality educational videos available throughout the school districts, thanks in equal measure to compression technology, innovation, and vision:

> In 1985, I founded Library Video Company, which quickly grew into becoming the largest video distribution company to K-12 schools and libraries in the United States, with VHS and Beta tapes—the only formats available at the time. As a mail-order distributor, I wanted to give the company an edge with superior proprietary content created specifically for schools and libraries as opposed to television programs. So, in 1990, I formed Schlessinger Media, producing K-8 educational video programs directly aligned to the curriculum by grade and subject matter. We produced 23-minute-long programs to fit neatly into a class period, in both English and Spanish, with closed-captioning and teacher's guides.
>
> We found our voice as a multicultural content-focused publisher, first adapting a book series from Chelsea House Publishers, then producing editorial content from scratch. In all, we produced about 700 programs. In retrospect, video didn't really make sense for a school district curriculum in those days for two main reasons:
>
> 1. Video in a physical form, including DVD, typically meant each school purchased just one copy, so a teacher had to reserve the program from the school library and show the video during class to all their students. That was a lot of wasted class time and limited the amount of relevant video content that could be used in a course.
> 2. Each school librarian was responsible for purchasing their own collection, so there was no consistency throughout a district as to what video content was available to all students at any time.

For example, a school could not assign 30 students in their class to watch the same video as homework in advance of a class. This also evolved into a problem of equity, with some schools in a district having access to more video resources than others.

Throughout the 1990s and early aughts, all the major educational publishers added video to their offerings and licensed Schlessinger Media videos to accompany their texts. However, this still didn't resolve the limiting factor for scaling the use of video because there was just a single physical copy of a video for an entire class or school.

When the Internet came along, initially bandwidth was a major challenge for video playback in schools. Video on a screen was postage-stamp sized, very grainy when enlarged, and used way more bandwidth and storage space than was practicable. The pioneers of early online educational video services, United Learning and Aims, called themselves *streaming* services, but the digital video had to be *downloaded* overnight for playback from a teacher's workstation the next day in class. It took years of improvements in video compression technology and broadband cost reductions before streaming video was ready for prime-time on-demand streaming in school district classrooms.

In 2005, Library Video Company/Schlessinger Media merged with SAFARI Technologies, a company founded by Tim Beekman, to become SAFARI Montage, with the fundamental premise to take a vast library of the best educational video resources, encode them for digital delivery, and add metatags so they could be searched, selected, and played seamlessly in a school or throughout the district.

A brilliant engineer and video network pioneer, Tim had developed a technology that alleviated the Internet bandwidth bottleneck that occurred in every district when video was being played back from the cloud by placing a server on the school or district premises to leverage their plentiful Wide or Local Area Network (LAN) bandwidth and to preserve their centralized Internet pipe for other uses. This meant that a single hosted digital video could be played to an entire class of students at home at the same time.

With these technologies in place, SAFARI Montage introduced the first K-12 educational Learning Object Repository (LOR) in the United States. Not only was the LOR filled with outstanding educational video, aligned to states' standards, but it allowed users to upload their own created content or compiled Internet links that they had found and curated. That content could then be shared with other users in the school or district, and playlists could be created to assemble content to support a lesson. As a foundation for video content that could scale to support a digital curriculum throughout a district, this was a huge moment in the evolution of the use of video delivery in K-12 education that occurred without much fanfare at the time but ultimately changed how a large percentage of courses were taught in the United States.

Now in 2021, major school districts have built lessons and courses using our Learning Object Repository as the base for media and proprietary digital content. Chicago Public Schools has launched their Curriculum Equity Initiative to provide every school and student in the district with a full digital curriculum. It's a major undertaking that has been years in planning and requires every educational publisher to build lessons and courses inside the LOR.

As I reflect over the years, I've seen times when content was king and others when the platform was the king, but truly it has always been that both components are equally essential to deliver a high-quality educational experience. If content isn't working at scale, seamlessly to all students, the quality of the content is irrelevant. If a delivery vehicle is flawless but is not open enough to access all content, it also is limited in its educational value. From the beginning of our video journey, we have made it a mission for SAFARI Montage to be focused on both, which has enabled us to develop a platform that worked seamlessly with any educational content provider.

Making it happen

When school buildings were shut down due to the 2020 pandemic, and teachers and students were sent home, remote learning became the norm. School administrators and teachers were caught without enough tools in their toolboxes to build a remote model that could work for their everyday responsibilities, and parents and students were unprepared and left without a manual on what their options were. EdTech companies, technology companies, non-profits, parent–teacher organizations, and other groups came up with a variety of disparate solutions. Given the varying problems and the unique situations, there was no expectation that a uniform response or solution would be possible. While there were myriad problems facing school districts and their constituents, the one problem that everyone faced was how to maintain a high level of education when neither the adults nor the children could be in school or have access to the tools that teachers and students normally depended on.

Phyllis Hillwig, CEO and Founder of Math All Around and Eurekii, decided to do something about it. She established a virtual learning center, where six- through nine-year-olds could join a Zoom session and have fun learning math through activities that relate to their everyday lives. Her activities involved sports, fashion, and nature walks where children were doing math but, as she puts it, "not seeing math." She created a virtual after-school club environment where kids were immersed in math and didn't realize it.

The usual places where they gathered—recreation centers, friends' homes, and even the park—were closed for Covid, so her idea was to fill the void with an alternate virtual reality. But she didn't stop at a Zoom call. She put the afterschool activities in a box, with engaging books and interactive videos that guided the kids through the activities. The strategy: Fun first, math second.

The product was a Covid solution in a kit that simulated the environments that they would normally get in school and after. The videos culminated in a kind of performance related to the activity themes: Mock fashion shows and Olympics, board games, and a shopping spree. The outcomes included improved financial literacy, character development, and real-world experience of the math all around them. With the emphasis on real-life learning, the program was designed to be led just as easily by a parent as a teacher.

Soon after the launch of the product, she caught the attention of an educational distributor in China who has since partnered with Phyllis to bring the kits to mainland China, in English.

The positive response to the programs has prompted Phyllis to begin the development of additional themes, like math in space, careers, art, design, camps, outdoors, airplanes, and climate. Next, she plans on building the same type of activities around science to include such topics as genetics, probability, and density. She even has plans to develop activities around the physics in lava lamps.

Phyllis' secret sauce was not just fun activities or being able to engage kids with activities that are relevant to their daily lives—all important attributes of a successful educational product. What stands out was the execution, the high-level of the production, and the bringing together of multimedia, print activities, and sound pedagogy in a box—with an option to conduct the same activities on video chat. It is a formula that will thrive well past the pandemic.

Me, myself, and I

Although the options that authors and publishers have for showcasing their ideas have increased dramatically with technology, most ideas start with the written page and end with a published work in print. The number of published books has been exploding since the beginning of the digital age. In the United States, more than 1.5 million books are published each year, and climbing; two-thirds of them are self-published titles, including reprints of public domain works and print-on-demand books.[2] Year on year for the last dozen years, thanks to the digital revolution, most of the growth in publishing is coming from self-publishers.

Still, most of the revenue is earned by the traditional trade publishers, and 80% of their revenue derives from celebrity authors—political, entertainment, even business—and popular authors. In short, a small number of the total number of titles published every year make money, and the percentage declines each year as more titles are published, increasingly by self-publishers.

The best-selling titles generally continue to sell over time, so that the top authors form a kind of super society of elites. The best-selling author of all time is William Shakespeare, followed by Agatha Christie, Barbara Cartland, Danielle Steel, Harold Robbins, Georges Simenon, Enid Blyton, Sidney Sheldon, J.K. Rowling, and Gilbert Patten. Although he has probably been at the top of the list for some time, Shakespeare's last play, *The Tempest*, was written 410 years ago; J.K. Rowling got in the top ten in less than 25 years; her Harry Potter books stand as the best-selling series of titles of all time.[3]

In modern times, excluding works that have fallen into the public domain, all these top sellers have been brought to market by traditional trade publishers. It is still the case today that best-selling authors are published by established trade publishers. But not always. Best-selling books like Lisa Genova's *Still Alice*, Amanda Hocking's *Switched*, and *The Martian* by Andy Weir were all self-published. Even Margaret Atwood's first book of poetry, *Double Persephone*, was self-published, as was E.E. Cummings' early work. Though difficult, it is possible for a self-published author to publish a book that can make it into the pantheon of best-sellers.

The production processes for working with an established trade publishing house versus self-publishing are not hugely different. The real difference is in the marketing, promotion, and sales of the finished product, and because of this, many authors are choosing to self-publish.

As a self-publisher using Amazon's Kindle Direct Publishing (KDP) or any one of many self-publishing platforms and services, the steps for getting a manuscript to press are no different from the processes and procedures that a traditional trade publishing house will use. Self-publishers bear all the production and printing costs, but they earn a much larger percentage of the royalty revenue, somewhere between 50% and 70% versus between 8% and 15%. Writers who choose to take the self-publishing route, have the option to do everything on their own or outsource a company to perform the various publishing services for a fee. Such companies offer a variety of services, from manuscript development to printing and e-book conversion. In addition, authors can purchase a variety of services à la carte: From book design, barcodes, and ISBNs to print-run management and press releases.

Some authors start out as self-publishers and with success move to an established trade house. Hugh Howey, author of the best-selling book *Wool*, which he first published using the KDP platform, famously made this leap. After a variety of successes with the title, including selling movie rights, he eventually published with Simon & Schuster for distribution rights in the United States and Canada and Random House Century for U.K. rights, retaining all e-book sales for himself. Today he is recognized as an advocate of the self-publishing phenomenon and a model success story.

On the other hand, some authors may start by publishing a book or series of books with an established trade publisher and find that they did not get the service, attention, or sales that they had expected, had the rights reverted to them, and then took the solo route.

Jennie Walters wrote a trilogy of "Upstairs/Downstairs"-type novels, under the series title "Swallowcliffe Hall," aimed at the tween/young adult (YA) market.[4] The books were published originally by one of the Big Five trade publishers.[5] Hers was a case study of what can go wrong in the publishing experience and how it can be made right, at least in this case.

Jennie is an experienced children's editor herself, but that alone did not help with the publisher. Her commissioning editor went on leave, the covers were dreadful, according to her, and the marketing effort was non-existent, so sales were sluggish.

Five years after the initial publication, sales had been so low that Jennie was able to get the rights reverted to her. She still believed in the potential of the novels and one year later decided to self-publish the books only on Kindle (KDP). Even though she was a publishing professional, she was not particularly tech-savvy, so it took her a week to format the books (which she says she can now do in a day). She also took new cover photographs and commissioned much more attractive cover artwork. She used the bit of light metatagging allowed on the Kindle format to make the obvious connection between her books and the then smash TV hit *Downton Abbey*, which was a logical marketing gambit that the original publisher did not take up, thinking the TV series would not be of interest to young readers.

Optimistically, she thought that she might sell a few hundred downloads—at most, maybe, a thousand or two. However, during the last three years, she has sold more than 40,000 e-books, and has written and published a fourth title in the series aimed specifically at adults, which has also been successful. Of course, we hear about E.L. James and Amanda Hocking selling millions of units, but Jennie represents a mid-list author who was able to break through the noise in the market and find a niche for her work after the original publisher gave up. And of the 40,000 units she sold, Jennie, as a self-publisher, retained all the profits instead of earning a 10–15% royalty rate from a publisher.

To understand her sales history in context, even at those modest sales levels, she is still in the top 1% of self-published authors on Kindle, and for her, this achievement has been transformational. Not only has it been a confidence builder, but she has been able to identify her true market. Yes, the YA readers constitute a portion of it, but mainly it is women of a certain age—three Americans to every one Brit—who want to curl up in front of the fire with a slice of British tradition.

Authors are very often the forgotten part of the transformation in publishing—where most of the books published every year are self-published—partly because content appears to grow on endlessly available trees. But the opportunities for authors to take charge of their fate instead of complaining, has been empowering. This does not, however, guarantee success, but it does alleviate the finger pointing and excuses.

The second life of Jennie's series was enabled by a distribution option that did not exist in the pre-digital era. After being disappointed by the traditional publishing system, she used technology to become a self-publisher and the Internet to provide distribution. Because of these new publishing "tools," she did not need anyone's permission to change course, nor was there an outside publisher or distributor to reject her.

While Amazon's main value propositions were fixing a problem in the supply chain and offering outstanding customer service, they also provided a means for willing authors to serve as their own publishers and distributors, and to take control of their publications' destiny.

Self-publishing tools, along with online distributors, have created a new opportunity for people like Jennie. However, there are other bumps in the road that Jennie, fortunately, did not encounter that self-publishers should consider. Marshall Ross, Vice Chairman and Chief Creative Officer at the Cramer-Krasselt advertising agency is also a science fiction author. Since he has been in the creative end of his business for more than 25 years, he did not hesitate to self-publish his first book. For him, even though he learned a lot from the experience, received excellent reviews on his book, and won several indie awards, he may not want to go it alone on his next manuscript. Here is why:

In space, the famous movie poster proclaimed, no one can hear you scream. It's true in the void of self-publishing too. To be sure, going it alone in publishing has its rewards. Independence, creative control, quick meetings. But like any entrepreneurial endeavor, it's lonely at the top.

And unfamiliar too. Because once you've made the decision to self-publish, it's suddenly no longer about writing a book. Or even making one (which is easier than it seems). It's about selling a book. And that means doing one of the hardest things there is to do:

Build an audience. A thing most authors have never had to do as a collaboration with other people, let alone all alone.

I was lucky to have had some advance training before my leap. I've spent most of my career in advertising and the ad agency business had long ago transitioned away from just leveraging the audiences created by legacy media platforms, like the networks, to creating brand-based media platforms of our own. One of my clients has more Instagram followers than Disney's *Star Wars* franchise. And with the help of those "owned" media channels, we've been able to launch branded content series and other programming that often pull better numbers than the typical network sitcom.

The side of the industry that most profits from self-publishing, Amazon, and the proliferating world of author services and *Kindleprenurship* gurus, will have you believe attracting an audience is easy. Don't believe them. Even with my background in creative development and marketing, building traction behind my book was still a challenge. And I'm not ashamed to say it. Because it's hard for everyone. Even the big five publishers.

While the digitization of the book business lowered the barriers to entry (Yea!), it also multiplied the challenge for everyone to get seen. (F*ck!)

That's why the people most likely to get their work traditionally published are those with their own built-in audience bases or selling platforms outside of the world of books. They've already found success in TV or radio or online. More and more, the big five don't want to be in the audience building business. In today's *content-verse*, it's simply much easier, and far cheaper, to feed an existing audience than create a new one.

The difficult truth is unless you're already a personality with a following, when you finally launch your book, it will appear in the vacuum of distribution like a tiny star in the night sky. One of the unnamed billions.

But it is possible to make your star shine just a little brighter. I helped my little book beat the odds of obscurity by approaching my story not just as a writer but as a businessperson. I treated the project like I was launching a property rather than just a book.

I built a website that looked more like the launch of movie than an author's site. I did everything I could to expand my social graph prior to launch. I planned for both launch and sustaining activities.

And most important, I invested countless hours in deciphering the arcane and stubbornly mysterious world of Amazon Marketing Services, which I'm quite sure is where all the former leaders of the Soviet Union went to work. AMS is the part of Amazon that helps your book get seen on Amazon. It's where all those "Sponsored Products" come from. It's why your Kindle has ads on its screen even while it's sleeping.

AMS markets itself as a simple solution. A do-it-yourself solution. But it's about as do-it-yourself as a wall-to-wall bookcase from IKEA. It'll have you swearing right out of the blocks. Yes, you can use it in a simple way. The way AMS coaches. But you won't get the results you want unless you do more. Much more. One example: Amazon advises you to pick seven targeting keywords to embed in the metadata that direct what it calls a campaign, which is really just AMS speak for ad. In truth, you need hundreds of keywords to produce real results. And how do you find these keywords? If AMS knows it isn't telling. I think that's the business model. Let you learn by trial and error. Let you learn by spending. I have more than 20 years in the ad business and it took me five test campaigns to finally get it working.

The one saving grace of the thing is the reporting. The dashboard, though insanely hard to get to, is a good one. It's not too different from the kind my own agency provides our clients. But, again, it takes time to digest and manage. Lots of time. You can't get lazy with it. You have to optimize, optimize, optimize.

You,

you,

you.

This is the thing I've learned most about self-publishing. It's not we-publishing or us-publishing and it's certainly not them-publishing. It's you-publishing.

If you're up for it, the rumors you've heard are true. You can make it work. Especially if your book is good. You can keep more of the royalties from your work. And you will have the independence you crave. Along with the pride of having done it yourself.

But you do lose the chance to blame a disappointing performance on the publisher. Because, um, that's you.

Self-publishing is an option made possible by the digital era. It can create opportunities for new voices to be heard. As an alternative model, it does not compete with traditional publishing. There may be an argument that traditional publishers generate more successful titles. So far that seems to be the case. The market, and merit, will cause the cream to rise to the top, regardless of how it is generated.

Notes

1. "The Ears Have It: The Rise of Audiobooks and Podcasting," *Deloitte Insights*, December 9, 2019.
2. From Out: Think, March 4, 2021. https://outthinkgroup.com/the-10-awful-truths-about-book-publishing/. "The 10 Awful Truths about Book Publishing," Steven Piersanti, President of Berrett-Koehler Publishers.
3. These figures are not exact because for some books the data is not complete. According to some sources, excluding the *Bible*, *Don Quixote* is the best-selling single title of all time, but that includes both the original Spanish version and translations.
4. A version of this anecdote appears in *Dealing with Disruption*.
5. The "Big Five" publishers customarily refer to Penguin/Random House; Hachette Book Group; Harper Collins; Simon and Schuster; and Macmillan.

8

"PALACES FOR THE PEOPLE" AND THEIR TREASURES

> Libraries are not made, they grow.
>
> —**Augustine Birrell**

In his book *Palaces for the People*, Eric Klinenberg suggests that the future of democratic societies depends not only on shared values but on shared spaces: The libraries, childcare centers, churches, and parks where crucial connections are formed.[1] The title of his book is taken from Andrew Carnegie's description of the thousands of libraries that he had built and funded. At the turn of the 20th century, Carnegie, then the richest person in the world, sponsored the building of 1,689 public libraries and more than 100 academic libraries in the United States, 660 in Britain, and many more throughout the Commonwealth. A century later, Bill and Melinda Gates picked up the same philanthropic torch with the creation of the Gates Library Foundation in 1997, which has provided grants to more than 5,800 libraries in the United States and Canada earmarked for increasing bandwidth and digital content.

DOI: 10.4324/9781003162636-9

While it may seem surprising that print has survived (and continues to thrive) with little change for more than 600 years, the library's enduring presence speaks volumes about our cultural values. At least 3,000 years before Gutenberg's printing press made the replication of books possible, Eastern and Western societies have had libraries of one kind or another. From the Latin *librarius*, meaning relating to books, libraries have been iconic cultural structures from ancient through modern times, literally pillars of our civilization and as indispensable to our towns and cities as schools and fire stations. Serving as a permanent place for organizing, collecting, sharing, and storing documents, books, and even tablets (stone, not electronic), the library has not strayed far from its original mission over the centuries. While its main function as a repository of knowledge and a communal hub for learning has not changed, the library has evolved to embrace technology, providing patrons free access to seminal scholarly, literary, and creative digital works. We can say with certainty that technology has not made the library obsolete but has empowered it to become an essential influencer, curator, and knowledge provider in the digital age. The library may be more relevant today than it has ever been.

A decade ago, I served briefly on the board of a local university that was in the process of building a new library in the center of the university's quad. It was designed to be a high-tech showpiece for learning and collaboration with a major initiative to digitize the university's proprietary, scholarly documents collection. During a discussion concerning the name for the library, one board member questioned why we should continue to use the name "library" if the intention had been to phase out physical books. He suggested calling it a media or knowledge center. In fact, the objective was to add digital books to the collection, not de-emphasize or halt the acquisition of physical books—the architectural plans for the new building had allotted enough shelf space for the university's current collection as well as additional room for future acquisitions. (In all fairness, though, space for physical books is a problem for all libraries and one reason why they are ramping up their e-book collections.) Looking back at it today, "library" was the right moniker—and given its longevity, probably always will be. With apologies to Shakespeare, books by any other name would mean the same.

Total product acquisition in all three primary library segments—public, school, and academic—still tilts in favor of physical books, but with greater annual increases in spending for e-books. We do find, however, variations in buying behaviors among the three segments due to differences in budget size and constituent priorities.

In 2019, roughly 60% of total collection expenditures in the public libraries in the United States were devoted to printed books and 20% for electronic materials, including e-books, audiobooks, e-serials (journals), database licenses, reference tools, musical scores, maps or photos in digital formats, as well as materials digitized by the library and held both locally and remotely for which permanent or temporary access rights have been acquired; and another 20% for "other materials," such as microform, audio CDs, video, and DVDs. Except for audio files, these formats, often described as "new materials," have become mostly obsolete. The acquisition of digital content has been growing faster than physical content, but public libraries have been building their e-book collections in earnest for only a little over a decade.[2] On average, there is a 70/30 split between physical and digital formats with trends in annual budgets that are gradually closing the gap in spending differences between the two.

We find a similar trend in school libraries, where e-book purchases are increasing at a higher rate than physical books and represent approximately 35% of their budgets. The amount of funds that schools devote to purchasing or subscribing to digital products and online websites correlates with the time students spend with technology-driven learning tools. Classroom and study time with online content has been increasing over the years and represents roughly 30–35% of students' total study time. The 2020 pandemic caused a sudden and dramatic shift to digital learning solutions, which will likely result in an even greater role for online learning once schools reestablish in-building teaching. So as not to return to the way things were prior to the pandemic, school reform advocates are pressing for more online and remote learning to become permanent parts of the daily curriculum, making greater use of blended learning, and flipped classrooms.[3]

At academic libraries, we find a proportionately greater use of technology than in either the public or school sectors, which corresponds to the ubiquitous use of technology in college and university classes. Of the approximately $2.8 billion that academic libraries spent in 2019 on information resources, half of those expenditures were for current electronic serial subscriptions. In one recent report on the purchasing patterns in academic libraries, "expenditures made for print books obtained on a one-time, title-by-title basis decreased year to year, while e-book expenditures obtained in the same way experienced a net increase."[4]

Palace squabbles

For almost the entire history of the library ecosystem, publishing companies and libraries have been as tightly aligned in their missions as any other pair of mutually beneficial partnerships. It is hard to imagine a more symbiotic relationship than that between publishers and libraries. The two entities appear more interdependent than baseball bat manufacturers and professional baseball teams; coffee bean growers and Starbucks; music recording studios and radio; or mini-series producers and Netflix. The relationship between publishers and libraries had been wrinkle-free for more than a hundred years, based on a simple model: Librarians purchase new and evergreen books from the publishers, catalog the books in their system, arrange them on shelves, and loan them out to their patrons for free for a prescribed length of time. If a particular title happened to be exceedingly popular and became a best-seller, librarians might buy multiple copies so as not to keep patrons waiting too long for an opportunity to borrow the book. This arrangement appeared to be entirely uncontroversial—until e-books came along and caused some publishers to question whether the model for supplying physical books to libraries could be applied to e-books. Some publishers believed that they and their authors were not getting the same value from e-books as they were from the sale of physical books, and, moreover, that the availability of e-books in the library market was directly affecting print sales, causing a net loss in revenue.

When a librarian buys an e-book, rather than having a physical book to put on a shelf, the digital "copy" resides as a file in the library's database. Patrons borrow the books as digital downloads on their computer or e-reader, but the original digital book remains in the system and, depending on the downloading permissions that were previously negotiated between the library and the distributor/publisher, could be borrowed an unlimited number of times by other patrons. To create a model that more closely resembles how libraries purchase and loan physical books, publishers use digital rights-management (DRM) algorithms to put a usage limit on borrowing permissions. While an e-book is on a time-limited loan to a patron, the file is "locked" until it is "returned" or when the pre-set loan time expires. Librarians could, in theory, buy more than one license to a title, but the cost for adding additional licenses is not typically in the library budget, particularly since there is no way of knowing what the demand for any given title will be. As we know, even with physical books, some titles are constantly in circulation while others just sit on the shelves and get little use. For any given title, publishers could, in theory, raise the cost of the e-book license, extend the permissions to include more than one borrower at a time, or even allow for unlimited, concurrent use. But for single standalone books, the typical model that librarians prefer to use for their budgets is one borrower at a time, which is consistent with the way physical books are managed.

In the summer of 2019, some trade publishers were concerned that releasing new e-book titles to libraries simultaneously with their release to the retail trade would cannibalize their sales. They worried that readers would borrow the e-book from the library instead of buying the book. Thus, they instituted a policy to delay the e-book release of new titles to libraries until eight weeks after the publication date. The libraries could buy the print version on publication, as usual, but the publishers would retain all e-book sales for their retail distributors and their own websites during the so-called embargo period.

Tensions rose so high when this policy was first introduced, that the headlines in articles about the publisher–library relationship verged on the toxic. Articles appeared in industry publications with titles like "Are Publishers for or Against Libraries?"[5] Librarians had the impression that a few publishers wanted to punish libraries and their patrons, traditionally the publishers' biggest advocates, without evidence that their sales would be negatively affected. Librarians felt as if their "palace for the people" was under siege.

From the publishers' point of view, they were being proactive out of concern for possible revenue losses if they continued to allow library patrons free and easy access to their front-list titles during the early days of a new title launch. They thought that they were acting on behalf of their authors and were putting typically strong early sales of new releases at risk if library patrons could download e-book versions for free. However, the eight-week delay policy came from only a hunch about the potential loss of revenue not from the data. (A small number of publishers have gone even further than instituting moratoriums by withholding e-books from library sales altogether).

Librarians have a different view. First, they consider themselves loyal paying customers, and are prepared to pay for e-books just like physical books; and second, by making new titles available to their patrons, in all formats, they are functioning as a kind of marketing arm for authors and their publishers.[6] In addition, they have more than anecdotal evidence that patrons who frequently use the library and borrow the most books also tend to buy the most books.

Not all publishers instituted an e-book moratorium on libraries, but often e-book availability still lags behind print. Further, depending on the library, all three book formats—print, e-book, audiobook—are not always available for all titles; the reason may be on the publisher's/distributor's end or due to the library's limited budget.

Most publishers have excellent relationships with libraries and do not view them as competitors but rather as arguably the most efficient and effective vehicle for raising awareness of new titles and promoting reading. The issue around e-books arose because of their novelty—as digital files they do not look like physical books on a shelf—and the unknown effect they may have on the introduction of new titles into the market. So, some publishers chose to take a conservative tack and not risk losing revenue. Indeed, a percentage of readers may borrow or download books instead of purchasing them, but chances are if they did not borrow them, they would not purchase them—or perhaps not even know about them—at all. In an interview published in a recent article in *Publishers Weekly*, the executive editor of the *Library Journal* revealed data from a survey that they had just conducted on library patrons' book-buying habits:

> Our data show that over 50% of all library users report purchasing books by an author they were introduced to in the library. This debunks the myth that when a library buys a book the publisher loses future sales. Instead, it confirms that the public library . . . is an active partner with the publishing industry in building the book market, not to mention the burgeoning e-book market.[7]

In short, if frequent library-goers borrow a book and like it, they are more likely to buy a copy, if not for themselves then as a gift—or recommend it to others, or better yet share their enthusiasm on social media and demonstrate the power of word of mouth.

Digital publishing has helped publishers expand their options for reaching a wider audience. Innovative digital formats for books and informational websites on general and specialized knowledge are being well received, giving readers access to more curated information from more sources. The e-book market is mostly additive and has attracted new readers into the market rather than siphoning off buyers of either physical books or audiobooks. It is a cliché to say that we need to "meet customers where they are," but this is precisely what published works in multiple digital formats has enabled publishers to do. Because of the various ways to repurpose and reuse digital content, publishers can create new products from their existing intellectual property (as well as develop new content) and reach just about anyone at any time, allowing readers to choose among a variety of formats based on their personal interests and preferences.

The unstable pricing terms for digital content, especially e-books, are teething pains for publishers as they experiment with a relatively new medium and how to best serve their customers—libraries and individual consumers—while maximizing their ROI. Physical books are sold, bought, and consumed as individual units, like bottles of water. Although e-books can also be consumed one download at a time, a single e-book file can potentially serve an unlimited number of users. But they can also be aggregated in a database and instead of being sold by the drink they can be licensed to institutions—libraries, schools, and universities—as water from a pump, and purchased through subscriptions like streaming services.

Although they may not alleviate the perception that e-books cannibalize publishers' sales, subscription models are gaining popularity and have the upside of avoiding individual e-book pricing. Over time, renewable subscription licensing models may help publishers earn more revenue from any given title than they would from a one-time purchase. Libraries are allocating an increasing percentage of their budgets to subscriptions to databases. Since they can track how much usage databases receive, librarians can spend their funds on products that are being used the most instead of owning products that are rarely used or not used at all.

Given the fluctuating purchasing and licensing models for various online products, libraries must adjust their budgets and buying processes. Because of annual renewal rates, subscription models compel libraries to allocate more funds to the maintenance of existing collections over the acquisition of new content. According to some estimates, 25% of library budgets are spent on re-purposing existing content instead of acquiring new content.

Even so, budget redistribution seems to be steering libraries in the right direction, providing patrons with the access to the books, information, and knowledge that they want and use the most.

It will take time to gather and analyze data on buying vs borrowing behavior before settling on the ideal model that will benefit all interested parties equally. In the meantime, we should continue to expect more experimentation with pricing models and, perhaps, new-title release embargos of one kind or another.

Keys to the kingdom

In 2012, while I was at Britannica, I started an e-book product line for the K-12 institutional and library markets. That was the same year that we sold our last print set of encyclopedias. I had developed approximately 200 books on a variety of curriculum topics, drawn principally from content in our database. We had issued some of the titles in print several years earlier, but we stopped reprinting those titles when the decision was made to retire the print set for good. The e-book business was just gaining traction, and I had a half dozen e-book distributors promoting and selling to the school library market. The 200 books were a decent start, but I wanted an ongoing publishing program with a strong backlist and a fresh front list, with the goal of launching 75–100 new titles each year.

I partnered with a well-respected educational publisher who was willing to jointly develop new titles from our database and split distribution rights by format; we granted them worldwide print rights and kept all digital rights for ourselves, including e-books. Starting with a well-curated, authoritative database saved both of us time and resources and enabled us to push product into our respective pipelines much faster. We agreed on co-publishing approximately 100 new titles a year that would be sold in library bindings by their full-time sales representatives and distributors and that I would use to expand my e-book program, splitting distribution along our separate marketing channels.

As the e-book market developed, e-book platforms grew in popularity. Buying behavior by school library systems started to shift in favor of subscriptions to e-book database platforms over individual e-books sales. To consolidate a database of our e-book titles with consistent functionality across all titles—like bookmarking, highlighting, and search capabilities—I licensed a white-label platform from a software company that we customized to create a market-differentiated experience. While our individual e-book titles still sold into the handful of crowded distributors' databases with hundreds of thousands of other titles from hundreds of publishers—and sold into the customers' systems, which in the school library market was mostly EBSCO or Follett—the value of our e-books increased dramatically within our customized platform. The platform allowed us to curate and select titles to our customer's specifications and create unique packages with subject-specific titles targeted to the elementary-, middle-, or high-school market. Because we could align books specifically to user needs, the e-book platform raised the value of the individual titles as well as the entire collection in the database.

After five years developing the e-book title list and tweaking the platform, we had almost 1,000 titles in the database and a responsive platform with functionality based on customer feedback and specific requests, like integration with the most popular LMS platforms; all-device performance (in responsive design); Single-Sign-On (SSO) capability; classroom rostering; formative and summative assessment; curriculum standards and Lexile alignment; and, most importantly, detailed usage reports. With a robust title list and a full-featured e-book platform, we were able to meet the requirements of several state- and district-wide RFPs. One of the most extensive was a Texas statewide RFP for hundreds of elementary-level titles on literacy and science. The RFP specified unlimited, simultaneous usage for all classrooms in all 7,800 elementary schools in the state.

We won the RFP and negotiated a five-year renewable license of approximately 500 titles. After year one, a review of the usage statistics was conducted to determine whether there was enough engagement across the state to justify renewing the license for a second year. Once that was confirmed, the data from the usage statistics helped to determine which titles were the most popular and which received little use. For year two, we kept the most popular titles on the platform but swapped out the titles that showed little or no usage and replaced them with either new titles that we had published during the past year or other titles from our database that the customer had selected as the most relevant replacements.

For the educators and the curriculum directors in the state, the most important metric in determining the value of the platform was whether usage on the platform went up over the term of the license. They had an annual per-student budget, and they wanted to spend it on titles that students and teachers valued and spent time on. If, with the same budget, they had purchased randomly selected print books instead of licensing our e-books, they would be stuck with some number of books that no one used. In addition, they would have to buy classroom sets of the same title if they wanted all the students in a class to work with the same books at the same time. With our e-book platform, one digital file of a title could be used simultaneously by every student in all 7,800 schools. For these reasons, the annual license—which allowed every student access to the same books and gave the state buyers the opportunity to replace any number of titles for the renewal period—was a much better value than wasting money on physical copies of books that may not have met their needs.

Ian Singer, the CEO of LibraryPass—a curator and distributor of high-interest, digital content for K-12, public, and academic libraries—believes that usage should be the number-one metric for establishing customer value of titles—or databases—that libraries acquire. He also believes that publishers must help make their online products easy to use:

Speaking specifically about the education/library markets (B2B vertical), Covid-19 exposed the risks of not having a coherent digital publishing strategy. Aside from the digital divide issues (which are significant), there is now no question that technology will continue to disrupt positively the library marketplace. Acceptance of digital learning and communication applications, as well as content and services that engage readers and patrons will continue to accelerate.

The key is to ensure usage. Educators and librarians are constantly bombarded by new products and services to offer; as such, publishers need to take certain measures to deepen the reading experience—and thus usage—by not worrying about the sales their titles are generating but rather focusing on how well their content renders [on a platform] and whether it can be included in shared-interest reading groups and programming.

Experimenting with access models is critical; so, if your content cannot be shared, how can it be used, affordably, in educational settings like English classes or public library reading groups? At LibraryPass, we work (for now) to license content that fits only into a simultaneous use, unlimited access model precisely to enable educators, librarians, and readers to have less access-friction, easier discovery, and shared reading experiences.

The state of Texas renewed our e-book collection for five more years (it was still in place when I left the company), primarily because we had continued to swap out titles after each renewal period, which positively affected the overall usage on the platform. The unlimited concurrent use license, which was specified in the RFP, provided us with the best way to demonstrate a high level of engagement with the platform and therefore justification for renewal.

After meeting or exceeding customer expectations, it is up to the publisher to arrive at a pricing structure (which I discuss in the next chapter) that is mutually beneficial and raises the average customer lifetime value.

Trusted sources

When the pandemic hit like a tsunami in February–March of 2020, traveling against the weather patterns from the east to the west, few institutions proved to be as resilient and relevant as the library. Businesses shut their doors and had their employees work from home; restaurants either went out of business or stayed open only for take-out service; and most schools and universities went into a full or partial state of remote learning. But libraries remained open for business. Although you could not enter the buildings—and in-person activities like makerspaces were put on hold—the main library services continued to operate, and anyone with a library card could take advantage of the services for free. Even popular "escape rooms" went virtual at many public libraries.[8]

Our family of five—three children with a teacher/editor mother—have always been frequent library users. But like many people, I relied on the library much more during the pandemic, in part because I was still researching this book, but also because I had more time to spend catching up on my reading and learning about new or upgraded features in the software applications that I use every day. I prefer to read physical books over e-books if they are available, and just as I have always done, I was able to reserve them seamlessly during the pandemic through my library's website. After I put in my request, I would be notified by e-mail when the books were ready to pick up at the designated "safe" area of the building, which was conveniently located next to the library's parking lot; if I opted for curbside pickup, a librarian would bring the books to my car. I returned them to the customary book-return bins just outside the building.

Once logged in to the library's website, I had access to the digital newspaper and magazine archives; current online journals; and business, health, and reference databases. I downloaded e-books with Overdrive's "Libby" app on my iPad, took advantage of the extra "pandemic" time I had by taking four asynchronous online courses, and watched movies through the library's licensing arrangement with the Kanopy and Hoopla media databases.

Our library, in suburban Chicago, did not have to interrupt hardly any of its services during the pandemic while the building itself was closed, as its physical and digital resources are no longer confined within the walls of the library building. Because most of the library's services are available online, the library acts mainly as a kind of server farm and conduit to the cloud. Moreover, our small library is part of a larger network, or consortium, of 26 suburban libraries, which together serve a population of approximately 800,000, providing the level of resources—total number of physical books and online databases—of a medium-sized city. Any member library and their patrons with Wi-Fi access can tap into the same online network of 26 sites. Even physical books, when reserved online, can come from any of the sites and be delivered to the member's home library for pickup.

As a consortium, the library network has the buying power of a city library. The online resources are licensed by a committee appointed by the consortium, not by the individual libraries. Conveniently, publishers' representatives and their distributors need to make only one sales call to service all 26 libraries and can work with a much bigger budget as a result. Acting as a single buyer, the library consortium can take advantage of economies of scale. These types of library networks have become a nationwide trend—evidence of how well libraries have leveraged digital content and contribute to 21st-century learning. Clearly, libraries are much more than warehouses for books.

A recent article in the *New York Times* about the future of libraries credits libraries with their readiness to serve when the pandemic hit:

> Many companies and public institutions were unprepared for the pandemic and the ensuing lockdown. There was one notable, perhaps even

surprising, exception: The nation's public libraries. With a wealth of electronic books, streaming platforms and of course Zoom, many were ready, with some adjustments, to provide services for their communities. But no one could have predicted that 2020 would create the moment when 'our libraries, the most trusted civic institutions in the country, would become totally virtual,' said Anthony Marx, the president and chief executive of the New York Public Library, the nation's largest library system after the Library of Congress.[9]

The library's ability to carry on its mission was in large part due to the work that publishers have done to digitize their content and create new products and services; publishers have been converting their older formats into digital assets over the last 15–20 years and using digital platforms to make access to individual components easier to find, use, and monitor. But making these efforts available and of value to patrons required the vision of library leaders to embrace these products and services and put in place the technology—and skilled knowledge professionals—necessary to deliver them.

Libraries have been most aggressive in building their digital offerings in three main product categories: Media (e-books, e-audiobooks, e-zines, movies, music, and TV shows); Online Databases; and Online Courses. Below are screenshots of these category offerings from my library's website:

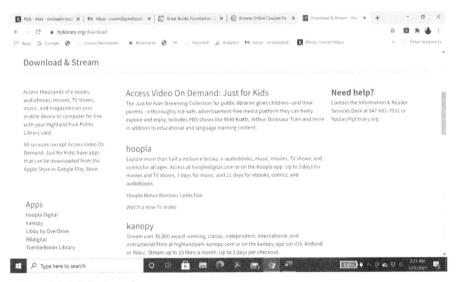

Figure 8.1 Media Interface.

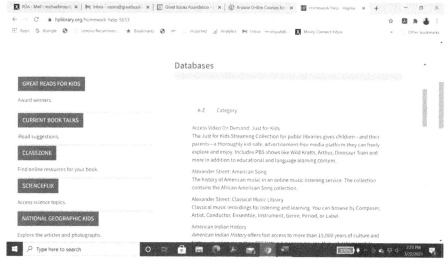

Figure 8.2 Database Interface.

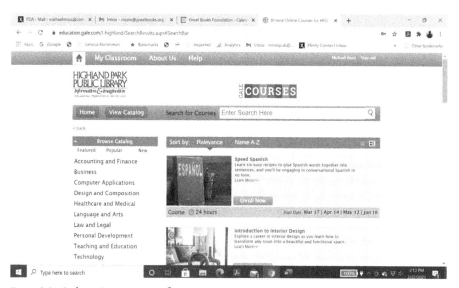

Figure 8.3 Online Courses Interface.

Media has been a mainstay of libraries for more than 30 years and the digitization of the offerings has largely replaced the older formats—cassette tapes, CDs, and DVDs. Online databases and online courses are products of the 21st century, powered by technology and enhanced by continual innovation.

Much of the digital content provided by publishers and aggregators originally existed in an analog format and had been converted to digital formats over time. (Hoopla, for example, is the digital media service arm of Midwest Tape, which still sells shelf-ready DVDs, Blu-rays, and physical audiobooks.) However, an increasing number of digital products have been developed exclusively for the online environment without a legacy format.

Usage statistics from online products provide valuable data to publishers. Even though there is never a guarantee for success, by capturing usage data, publishers can develop more targeted products based on user behavior—what they frequently search for and spend time on—rather than their opinions on surveys. In this way, usage of digital products in the library can substitute for focus groups for validating the general direction for future product development.

Markets are still segmented, meaning not all digital products are suitable for all markets. Product requirements and functionality in the education market are quite different from the consumer market. The library market may seem closer to the education market, but it tends to be more of a cross between the consumer and education market, depending on the product category, with its own characteristics and preferences. Publishers generally have separate divisions to serve these markets with different product lines, though some products can be adapted for more than one market. It is unlikely that any product can be successful in all three markets without significant adaptation. With a focus only on digital assets, EdTech publishers can meet the needs of both the school and library markets with minor adaptations and an incremental investment relative to the cost of the initial product development.

At Britannica, we created four separate products from the same database: Consumer, school, public library, and academic library. Moreover, the school product featured three different interfaces—elementary school, middle school, and high school. The public library and consumer products sported a separate junior and adult interface. The academic interface featured links to scholarly journals, research tools, and provided access to a separate primary sources database. The consumer product was further segmented to accommodate either an ad-based or subscription-based revenue model. Each product had different features specifically geared to its respective market, but they all drew from the same database and software platform. We leveraged as much content and widgets as we could. Although repurposing digital assets was not free, we were not starting from scratch for each product iteration, and we were able to carve significant market share in each of the channels.

Last year I worked with an all-digital curriculum publisher whose products were designed specifically for the middle- and high-school classroom, with separate platform views for teachers and students. The CEO of the company asked me to prepare a product and marketing plan that would enable them to effectively sell the same titles to the library market, for which they had no current products. The courses were self-paced, asynchronous, and included feedback loops (self-check quizzes), interactive activities to check comprehension, and live actor (as opposed to machine-generated text-to-speech) audio. We were able to design product plans to come up with two types of self-study library products: One was an audio version only, which required stripping out any visual content and adding pauses and section transitions to allow the listener to better retain the content aurally; the other fell neatly into the asynchronous online course category by eliminating any teacher-directed material and didactic language around testing or grades.

Although each of the new courses required some new development and editing, we were able to create templates without creating any new content assets, saving quite a bit of time and money. As derivatives of richly developed curriculum products, the new library products would have a much higher ROI and better margins than the original classroom products. Assuming the publisher had access to international markets, creating foreign-language versions would be another way to leverage the same content with minimal investments.

Notes

1. *Palaces for the People: How Social Infrastructure Can Help Fight Inequality, Polarization, and the Decline of Civic Life* (Crown, 2018).
2. According to the U.S. Government Publishing Office's (GPO) website, *Government Book Talk!* in 2009 Sony linked their e-reader with libraries that had adopted Overdrive's digital network, one of the first to enable library patrons to borrow e-books directly from their local library.
3. A flipped classroom is a kind of blended learning—partly online and partly in the classroom—where the student first studies the topic at home and problem-solves and collaborates in the classroom.

4. Katherine Daniel, Joseph J. Esposito, and Roger C. Schonfel. "Library Acquisition Patterns," *Ithaka S+R*. Last Modified 29 January 2019. https://doi.org/10.18665/sr.310937.
5. "Do Publishers Suddenly Hate Libraries," by Joseph Janes, in the August 16, 2019 edition of *Publishers Weekly*, discusses this controversy, which has not been entirely resolved. A small number of publishers continue to hold back their e-books from the library market.
6. A few years ago, my wife and I went to an informal discussion/interview at the Chicago Art Institute with Karl Ove Knausgaard, who had just published his fifth book in his six-book *My Struggle* series. He said that in Sweden, the government buys enough books by authors to put in all ~1,100 libraries in the country, for two reasons: It is a way to subsidize artistic expression, but also the library gives authors exposure that they would not otherwise get.
7. Andrew Albanese, "Survey Says Library Users Are Your Best Customers," *Publishers Weekly*, October 28, 2011. Also in the article is this quote from the Library Journal's *Patron Profiles*: "In addition to the billions libraries spend buying books, the data show those books in turn are spurring individual readers to buy more books."
8. According to the ALA:

    Escape/puzzle rooms . . . incorporate gamification into the library. These interactive live adventure games appeal to all ages and abilities and provide people with a chance to be a part of a story and their community as they problem solve.

9. Ellen Rosen, "Beyond the Pandemic, Libraries Look toward a New Era," *New York Times*, September 24, 2020.

9
"INFORMATION (ALMOST) WANTS TO BE FREE"

> What is a cynic? A man who knows the price of everything and the value of nothing.
> —**Oscar Wilde,** *Lady Windermere's Fan*, 1892, Act III

Apple's co-founder Steve Wozniak, and Stewart Brand, editor of the *Whole Earth Catalog*, had a conversation at the first Hackers Conference in 1984 where Brand famously said:

> On the one hand . . . information sort of wants to be expensive because it is so valuable—the right information in the right place just changes your life. On the other hand, **information *almost* wants to be free** because the costs of getting it out is getting lower and lower all the time.

To which Wozniak replied: "Information should be free, but your time should not."[1]

When we usually see Brand's quote reported, "almost" is not part of it, because, I suppose, whoever quoted it was an advocate for free information.

DOI: 10.4324/9781003162636-10

In any case, it is true that the cost of making information available is getting lower, if by that we mean the cost of bandwidth, storage, and the technology that provides the foundation for digital information and its transference. But as Wozniak reminds us, the time it takes to create information is not free, even if many of us are willing to create information without compensation. Publishers make significant investments to provide customers with curated, accurate, authoritative products, which, like any product or service of value, come with a price. In an ad-supported model, content—even authoritative, engaging content—can be free to the user since advertisers are footing the bill. And as we have been discussing, library patrons can get information for free because libraries are paying for it. But information does not want to be free; humans want information to be free. Everything has its price.

What price is right?

Pricing models for books and physical media (CDs, DVDs, audiocassettes) are straightforward, whereas the current pricing models for online content can be baffling—a mixed bag of sponsored content and motley subscription and licensing models, with little market consensus on what online access to various products should cost. Buyers favoring subscription models are motivated to eliminate advertising from their reading and searching experience. Still, some subscription products—like magazines and newspapers—contain advertising, though less of it than their free versions. Avoiding advertising may be an incentive to subscribe to a service, but it does not address the value proposition, or help to establish a pricing benchmark. Online pricing models vary quite a bit, especially when competitive products in certain subject areas give consumers multiple choices. With more specialized, or scarce information, where premium options are more limited—like financial or authoritative health information—we find less price variation.

For educational products, sold to schools, districts, states, and sometimes even countries, annual subscriptions are typically based on the population served, and an imputed price per user that the publisher and buyer agree upon. But there is no standard for this. I have made countrywide licensing deals with both small and large countries like Egypt, Wales, and Brazil that provide free access to a website for everyone in those geographical areas for a fixed price regardless of how much usage the website attracts. In each case, the negotiated price was primarily based on what the market would bear rather than any intrinsic value placed on the product's website or anticipated traffic. Even heavy user interest after the first year of service did not allow us to increase the price, though low usage usually meant that the price could be negotiated down, or the contract canceled.

Enormously successful subscription content sites like Netflix, HBO, *The Wall Street Journal*, *The New York Times*, and *Financial Times* use a standard consumer model—a fixed monthly fee for unlimited use—where the end-user and the buyer are one and the same. Consumers can evaluate the features and benefits of the competitive products, compare pricing, and pick the best options for themselves. With educational products, the end-users (students, teachers, patrons, et al.) are the beneficiaries of the subscription purchase but not the buyers. Institutional buyers have different motives in making their decisions as to which services to subscribe to, based less on the cost of the subscription and more on what they believe the value is to their constituents.

Below is a table that shows sample pricing models by market. The table may not include all possible variants, but it covers the ones that I have either used myself or encountered in the marketplace. The price associated with consumer models tend to be transparent—often advertised—and competitive, whereas it is difficult to compare prices for competitive products in the library and education market since they are rarely posted and often negotiable. Even highly competitive RFP bidding is normally sealed.

Here are explanatory notes on each of the models in the table.

Subscription 1: An annual fixed-price model can be used for any segment in the education market but is typically for large populations of users, especially multi-building districts, states, or even countries. The fixed price is based on an imputed price per user but is not specified. This model applies best to large product implementations and would provide unlimited user access during the term.

Subscription 2: A price-per-building model would apply to products that are relevant for all teachers and students in a building, like reference databases or e-book platforms.

Subscription 3: FTEs, or full-time equivalents, refers to student enrollment at the start of the school year. Whether the student population grows or shrinks over the course of the school year, the price stays the same for the subscription term. In this model, the number of FTEs would exclude teachers even though teachers would have full access to the product.

Subscription 4: This model applies to subject and grade-specific online programs, e.g., grade 7 STEM (science, technology, engineering, and math); teachers also gain access.

Subscription 5: A per-teacher price would apply to an online resource that a teacher might use to present materials to the class, like a lesson-plan database. The teacher FTE model covers the number of teachers at the start of the school year and would apply to online professional development or training for all participating teachers or staff.

Subscription 6: This model provides for discounts based on the total number of buildings in a district. Discount amounts increase with the number of buildings. This formula is used for large online implementations like core curriculum or e-book platforms.

Subscription 7: With this formula, only a fraction of the total population that a public library serves is used to calculate the final price, the assumption being that not everyone in a geographic location uses the library. For example, let us say an estimated 5% out of a population of 1,000,000 uses the library, and the product price per user is $1.00; the library would pay $50,000 to provide everyone with a library card free access for a year.

Subscription 8: A price-per-use model gives library patrons access to a large database of content, but the library pays only for what is used. This model is often applied to media websites, like movies, and usually limits users to a certain number of uses per month or a certain amount of time on the site. The PPU model can include all or part of a book/movie. Day or hourly rates are becoming increasingly popular in public libraries.

Subscription 9: A tier model segments a market by population, like school districts or towns. Tiered pricing for an online package of, say, 20 different courses could look something like this:

- Tier 1: For populations served < 100K (~$2,500)
- Tier 2: For populations served >100K and <500K (~$3,500)
- Tier 3: For populations served >500K and <1M (~$5,500)
- Tier 4: For populations served >1M (~$6,500)

Tiers can always be adjusted depending on the populations being served.

Subscription 10: This is a typical consumer model used commonly for a variety of online products, like newspapers, magazines, and streaming services.

Advertising: An ad-based or sponsored model allows free access for all users. The sponsor pays for the ad space in one of several ways: A fixed price, CPM (cost per thousand impressions), CPC (cost per clicks), or CPA (cost per acquisition). Each one has its pros and cons.

Rate/Time: This refers to a fee-based online course, webinar, or experience that starts at a given time and lasts for a period anywhere from one week to a few months.

Rent: Some online products—e-books, language courses, for example—can be downloaded (rented) from aggregators or directly from the publisher for short periods of time, a common model for cooking or do-it-yourself sites, for example.

In addition to the pricing variability of online products, inconsistency in access permissions is equally common—from full, unlimited simultaneous access; monthly download limits per license or per user; single-use or

Table 9.1 Sample Pricing Models

Model	Term	Payment Metric	Market
Subscription 1	Annual	Fixed price	Education
Subscription 2	Annual	Price per building	Education
Subscription 3	Annual	Price per student (FTE)	Education
Subscription 4	Annual	Price per classroom	Education
Subscription 5	Annual	Price per teacher or FTE	Education
Subscription 6	Annual	Price times # of buildings (# discount)	Education
Subscription 7	Annual	Population served (total * X%)*$	Library
Subscription 8	Annual	Price per use; metered; fixed price	Library
Subscription 9	Annual	Tiered; fixed price RE population served	Library/education
Subscription 10	Annual/Mo.	Fixed price	Consumer
Advertising	Open	Free	Consumer
Rate/Time	Calendar	Fixed price	Consumer/Library
Rent	Day/hourly	Fixed price	Consumer

multi-use licenses per product, to micro-charges based on a short amount of time spent on a site (kind of like a parking meter). Though not the most common option, multi-year licenses can be desirable for both the publisher and the user—the publisher collects several years' worth of revenue up front and, in exchange for locking in the renewal, the user is protected against price increases, which is often a win-win for the content or service provider and the user of indispensable subscriptions. For example, I pay my website hosting provider for three years of service in advance because I want to lock in my cost and, at the same time, I do not want my site to go down. I feel quite differently, however, about my cell phone carrier—I pay by the month with no long-term commitment. I would happily switch to a cheaper service because I am confident that it will not be any worse at a lower price and I would just as soon save the money and use video chat if possible—where I can hear, as well as see, the person I am speaking to.

* * *

It is difficult for institutional buyers of online products to know in advance how the products will be received before using them in a classroom setting for an extensive period. Unlike a book, which you can browse through and glean its contents and relevance in a short period of time, an online product requires much more scrutiny over a longer period with a cohort of potential users. For this reason, most educators tasked with picking online products will request a trial period to test the product, or even a semester- or year-long pilot to get as many students and teachers as possible to kick the tires. In fact, even if the prospect does not request a pilot or extensive trial period, the publisher should strongly suggest it. It will create goodwill and more loyal customers over the long run. Luckily, it is a lot cheaper for a publisher to equip a school with enough licenses to conduct a pilot than providing sample textbooks, as was done for print pilots in the past.

Similarly, freemium models in the consumer market are used to develop product awareness—giving potential customers a free period to test a product before committing to an annual subscription. A freemium period will give the consumer an ad-free experience to see exactly what the product will look like if they were to subscribe.

Freemium trials for individuals and trials and pilots for institutions are useful tools to build deeper awareness of a product prior to making a long-term commitment. Awareness tools and strategies are the front-end equivalents of usage statistics. If awareness helps to predict a product's value for the consumer and instill a level of confidence that the product is the right fit and will deliver on the promise, usage during the subscription period will either prove or disprove it.

Note

1. Joshua Gans, "'Information Wants to Be Free': The History of That Quote," *Digitopoly*, October 25, 2015.

EPILOGUE

Back to the future

In Memoriam
Charles Benton (February 13, 1931–April 29, 2015)

Located about 50 miles northwest of Wichita on the Arkansas River, the city of Hutchinson, Kansas—known as "Salt City" for its extensive labyrinth of salt mines—is the home of Underground Vaults & Storage (UV & S), one of the largest and most secure storage facilities in the world. A 60-year-old privately held company with more than 40 acres of storage underground, UV&S sits on the site of a former salt mine, 650 feet (58 floors) below the surface of the earth. Surrounded by a 400-foot-thick wall—and far from urban sprawl and potential natural disaster—UV&S is one of the best and safest places on earth (or under the earth) for storing documents, films, and other perishable materials vulnerable to time, temperature, humidity, and contamination. Enveloped in what is essentially a salt-rock womb, this expansive, naturally climate-controlled space can keep fragile materials from degrading for an exceptionally long time (but perhaps not forever).

UV&S has hundreds of storage areas and private rooms, or "vaults," of various sizes that businesses, museums, galleries, and even private collectors can rent for long-term storage of artwork, artifacts, film, filmstrips, videotape, photographs, negatives, documents, data tape, books, movie props, and even antique carriages that require a consistently cool and dry atmosphere.

Soon after the facility opened in 1959, film and television studios identified the underground salt mines as an optimal environment to archive movie films and television-show masters. The first Hollywood studio to secure a spot in the facility was Columbia Pictures, in 1965. Today, most of the movie studios rent space at UV&S, where they store original camera negatives and old film prints produced on celluloid nitrate and celluloid triacetate, which could deteriorate over time if not kept in a tightly controlled environment. Warner Brothers, for example, rents 15,000 square feet of storage space there—the equivalent of 12 football fields— with racks that go up about ten feet to the ceiling

The scent of film

On October 28, 2010, I visited UV&S with my friend and colleague Charles Benton. Charles, the son of William Benton (a former U.S. senator from Connecticut, founder of the Benton and Bowles advertising agency, and a quintessential Renaissance man of his times), was a retired past-president of the Encyclopaedia Britannica Educational Company (EBEC), a division of Encyclopaedia Britannica, which between 1940 and 1980 was "by far the largest and most respected educational motion picture producing and distributing organization in the world."[1]

Charles had led the production and sales of Britannica films during the 1950s and 1960s, and although he left the company in 1967 to start his own film distribution company, Film Inc., he remained passionate about maintaining the legacy of the Britannica films, which were produced at the highest production standards possible at the time and written and directed by a who's who of educational film royalty. These were high-budget productions on a wide spectrum of topics, including real-life stage performances of literary classics—Hamlet, A Doll's House, and The Cherry Orchard—with professional actors; real-time filming of natural phenomena—e.g., volcanoes, earthquakes, and tornadoes—animals in their habitats; country profiles; space exploration; and the daily lives of workers in the manufacturing, agricultural, and fishing industries, among many others.

EPILOGUE   163

Charles and I went to the Hutchinson salt mines, where Britannica has been renting a private vault, for a dual purpose: To confirm that the original film negatives and prints were usable, organized, and accessible; and to understand what it might take to remove them safely and transport them to a vendor who could convert the film to a digital format.

In the 1990s, Britannica editors had selected about 1,200 titles out of a total of about 2,500 films and made them available to the market first in VHS and then on DVD. Once the digital versions were created from the VHS copies, editors combed through them, identified the most evergreen and relevant content, and selected short clips to repurpose in Britannica's online products and websites. Although some of the films were 30-plus years old, they stood the test of time and brought realism to hundreds of articles in the Britannica database. However, Charles believed that Britannica could and should do more with the films than just grab random clips and slot them in with other content. Even though the clips undeniably enhanced the contents of the database, they still did not let users experience the full narrative arc and impact of the films. Charles's goal was for Britannica to create a library of new digital masters from the original 16-mm negatives that could be used for broadcast quality distribution, which was not possible to do from VHS copies. His vision for these classic films went beyond bits of media to sprinkle around a massive database of articles.

Figure E.1 UV&S Salt Mine. Author's Photo.

Charles and I were met at the UV&S facility by a supervisor who took us down the 650 feet to the vault storage area on a vertical freight elevator, which was the only way in or out of the salt mine. For most of the ride it was pitch black—you could not see your hand if you pressed it against your face—noisy, and slow, but after an eternal ten minutes, we arrived at the bottom of the mine without incident.

The Britannica vault was easy to find, well-lit and organized, which was a pleasant surprise to both of us. According to UV&S management, Britannica was one of their first customers, which gave them a prime location among the many premier film and television studios. But all their vaults were equally as tidy. A physical card catalogue (UV&S was strictly analog) provided a roadmap to the films, filmstrips, and even 16-mm projectors that neither one of us expected to find there. The vault supervisor let us freely open the film canisters and examine their contents.

In going through the collection, we were concerned that when we opened the canisters, we would discover that some of the films had developed vinegar syndrome, a common consequence of aging and deteriorating celluloid film that has been exposed to any number of sources of degradation, like heat (which releases nitrogen gases), photochemical exposure (sunlight), or moisture. Under some adverse circumstances, the celluloid nitrate film could even burst into flames. Since the complete collection of

Figure E.2 Entrance to the Britannica Vault at UV&S. Author's Photo.

Britannica films date back as far as the 1930s, many of Britannica's films in the vault would have been printed on celluloid nitrate film, which film production companies stopped producing in the 1950s and replaced it with non-flammable celluloid triacetate.

We randomly pored over the film canisters and discovered that the film was in near pristine condition. For each title, all the film elements were there—sound and visual prints were arranged side by side in separate canisters—and we detected no scent of vinegar anywhere in the room or when we opened the canisters. We did not have time to go through all of them, but we felt that we had examined enough of a sample to determine that if it were possible to transport them safely and at a reasonable cost—and if we could find a vendor who could create digital files from 16-mm negatives reasonably (not a simple proposition)—almost all the movies would be in a good enough condition to convert to digital masters.

Charles and I exited up the same freight elevator that brought us down. He was energized by the prospect of repurposing the films in their entirety for a digital movie platform. The films were, indeed, gems, and almost impossible to replicate today.[2]

Even before our visit to the salt mines, I had been working with Geoff Alexander, the director of the non-profit Academic Film Archive of North America (AFANA), on ways to increase awareness of the Britannica films.

Figure E.3 Charles Benton in the Britannica Vault at UV&S. Author's Photo.

AFANA's mission is to acquire, preserve, document, and promote academic films by providing an archive, resource, and forum for continuing scholarly advancement and public exhibition.³ Geoff did not have access to any of Britannica's 16-mm prints, but universities, libraries, and museums who knew about his organization would send him copies of movies on VHS. If the display rights to the movies were cleared, which was the case with any film that had gone into the public domain, Geoff would convert them to a digital file and upload them to the Internet Archive Site where anyone could view them for free. Whenever Geoff received a Britannica film, he would confirm with me that it had entered the public domain and if so, he would upload them. Working this way, we were able to get dozens of Britannica films online, but both Geoff and I knew this effort was just touching the tip of the iceberg. And we also knew that working from VHS copies would not produce adequate production-quality results for optimal viewing, nor would they substitute for true archival material, as VHS has become obsolete and the hardware that can play the cassettes gets scarcer by the day.

Charles had a real advocate in Geoff, even though Charles believed that as a complete collection, the Britannica films should reside behind a paywall as unique and irreplaceable examples of the high-water mark of educational film production rather than as spotty exemplars on the Internet Archive Site. Either way, the first objective would be to transfer the Britannica corpus directly from the 16-mm films into a digital format, which would result in a higher-quality output and far better user experience, whether a selection of the films could be viewed for free on the Internet Archive or as a comprehensive collection under a SaaS model. Charles viewed the Britannica oeuvre with the eyes of a marketer, while Geoff viewed the films through the lens of a non-profit. I was interested in fulfilling both missions if possible.

Digital now!

By the time Charles and I went to the salt mines together in the fall of 2010, he had long distinguished himself in both the private and public sectors as an innovator, leader, and champion of diversity in the fields of education, information, cultural media, and communications. After leaving Britannica in 1967, he went on to become president or chairman of various for-profit organizations, including Public Media, Inc., Films Incorporated, Lionheart Television, Inc., and Home Vision Entertainment. In 1981, he founded the Benton Foundation, a non-profit committed to bringing "open, affordable, high-capacity broadband to all people in the U.S. to ensure a thriving democracy." Over the following three decades, Benton and his foundation became internationally recognized as influential proponents of communications policies that unite people and communities by promoting "values of access, equity, and diversity."[4] I was honored to be present when, in 2012, Charles received the Everett C. Parker award in Washington, D.C., "given in recognition of an individual whose work embodies the principles and values of the public interest in telecommunications and the media."[5]

During his remarkable career, Charles received three presidential appointments. President Carter appointed him Chairman of the National Commission on Libraries and Information Science in 1978; President Clinton appointed him a member of the Presidential Advisory Committee on the Public Interest Obligations of Digital Television Broadcasters in 1997; and in 2012 President Obama appointed him to serve on the National Museum and Library Services Board. As a result of his national reputation and experience with public libraries and policies, Charles had established a close working relationship with James Billington, who in 2010 was in his 23rd year as the 13th Librarian of Congress.[6] Charles discussed the Britannica film collection with Billington and his ideas about digitizing them and preserving them for future generations. Billington suggested that Charles and I talk to the director of the Packard Campus of the National Audio-Visual Conservation Center (NAVCC) in Culpepper, Virginia—where the Library of Congress preserves and provides access to the world's largest and most comprehensive collection of films, television programs, radio broadcasts, and sound recordings in the world, which sounded to us like a possible solution and hopeful destination for our quest to digitize the Britannica films. Thus, in the spring of 2010, with an invitation from the presiding head of the Library of Congress in hand, Charles and I went to the sprawling, 45-acre Packard campus of the LOC to find out if they would be willing to do more with the collection of films than watch them age in the salt mines, where, though they might be preserved for some time to come, they are likely to be forgotten.

The NAVCC is where old film, TV programs, radio broadcasts, and sound recordings go to live. As a branch of the LOC, the NAVCC is sent all media that are being registered for copyright by producers of content from all over the world. The NAVCC records, stores, and preserves every submission, whether it is in an analog format or digital format as most submissions are today. But it is also, remarkably, a digital mirror image of the Hutchinson salt mines: An above-ground, state-of-the-art facility that has "globally unprecedented capabilities and capacities for the preservation and reformatting of all audiovisual media formats (including obsolete formats dating back 100 years) and their long-term safekeeping in a petabyte-level digital storage."[7]

Although the main building—with more than 90 miles of shelving for physical collections; 35 climate-controlled vaults for sound recording, safety film, and videotape; and 124 individual vaults for more flammable nitrate film—is not open to the public, thanks to the introduction from our sponsor, Charles and I were given a private tour of the facilities, where we were able to observe the steps in the process for accepting, storing, and digitizing old and new media. The digitizing process is time-consuming because it must be done in real time. For example, if a typical Britannica film is 40-minutes long, after set-up and preparation it would take 40 minutes to digitize; the actual playing time of the film cannot be sped up. Analog-to-digital conversions are constrained by the mechanics of the analog playback.

Unlike the salt mines, where the private vaults and storage areas are 56 floors below the surface of the earth, the 124 vaults of the NAVCC are on the top floor of the main building. Since the vaults cannot take advantage of a natural, climate-controlled environment, the atmosphere at the NAVCC is maintained by computers to a constant, perfectly dry, and cool climate optimized for film preservation. Being on the top floor, the vaults have an emergency ceiling-mounted exhaust system that operates by sucking out the oxygen from inside the vault to snuff out a nitrate fire that might start in one of the films. In this way, the balance of the films in the vault would not be damaged by the introduction of a chemical fire retardant (water would not work, in any case, since nitrate film will continue to burn when wet).

Our guide gave us permission to look inside a vault, so we randomly selected one out of the 124 that were occupied. As soon as we stepped into the room, Charles immediately noticed a few Britannica films, which he recognized by the designs on the canisters. It was a complete coincidence. Our guide had no idea where the Britannica films were stored and no clue as to what films were in the vault we entered. The films in the vaults are not arranged by producer or owner but by the date on which they were logged in at the LOC. The Britannica films that Charles noticed had been sent to the LOC by the company when they were first being registered for copyright. The LOC has computerized records of all submissions going back to the first one, so they could, if necessary, track where each film was stored. It was possible that the entire collection of Britannica films was there somewhere spread out among the vaults, but we were not sure. We still needed to do the custodial work on the prints in the salt mine.

The LOC will store and organize films that are sent to them for free. But if a film collection owner makes a request to have any of their films digitized, they charge to do it, which is done on a first-come, first-paid basis. Given their backlog of films to convert from the various studios and private collectors, if we sent them the Britannica films within a month or two, it might take the better part of a year before they would be able to start working on them with their current staffing levels. Using one digital converter, it would take them approximately 70 business days to complete, assuming that there was a total of 2,500 films in the collection at an average of 40-minute long apiece. Another possible option for getting the job done sooner would be for us to provide the staff to work on site. They said that they could have the equipment available at any time, but the labor cost would be our responsibility, which they said some companies do subsidize when they want the conversions as soon as possible.

If they ever run out of paying customers, they will start to digitize the films that have been in storage for free in the order in which the films were received at the facility. Possibly, if their funding and staff power were to increase, they might be able to operate at a faster pace by adding more digital converters. But at the current pace, it is likely that the films would remain in limbo for quite a while. Still, even without a firm schedule for conversion, the films were more likely to be better preserved in the NAVCC facility than in the salt mine—with a chance, though slim, of someday giving them a second digital life.

When Charles and I returned to Chicago, we talked to Britannica's owners about moving the film from the salt mines and having them stored at NAVCC with the goal of getting them digitized. If we did not want to hire staff to do the work, we could probably get moved up in the queue by using some of our LOC clout, but it would still be costly to remove the stock from UV&S and transport it across the country. We also acknowledged that we did not have a business plan for monetizing the films. Charles believed they had a market value and that we could establish a Britannica educational film network, like Turner Classic Movies, and possibly re-start the production effort to create new videos. I was not so sure; Charles had more passion—and much more nostalgia—than I had. As someone said though: Nostalgia isn't what it used to be.

In the end, the owners decided to stick with the status quo. If the films were not at risk of degrading any time soon in the salt mines—and they did not appear to be—rather than investing in moving the inventory from the mine, transporting them in a refrigerated truck across the country, and underwriting the digitization without a clear path to an ROI, they preferred to keep their options open and continue to pay the annual UV&S rental fee. That discussion took place 11 years ago, and as far as I know the film negatives are still resting on the shelves in the vault in the salt mine.

From tactile to digital

The digital era has provided us with more access to more information without losing or sacrificing much if anything. It has created more options for creating and accessing text and media and has made it possible to preserve a variety of content formats for the future when even more options are likely to become available. The digital era has been built on our collective literacy and has expanded our ability to consume and apply knowledge through digital literacy, requiring additional skills beyond reading, writing, and simple math.

To innovate we need to continue to leverage technology skills and develop additional means for accessing information and applying our knowledge. The 21st century learner needs to be digitally literate to access and process the great amount of information that is constantly being produced, to determine what information is trustworthy, and to make positive cultural contributions.

We have only experienced net gains from the technologies that we have employed at increasingly lower costs. We have retained print—the oldest technology we have for recording and consuming knowledge—because it can be stored safely for a long time, easily accessed by the largest number of people, and we have figured out how to continue to make it affordably and to use it practically. Books are a successful technology with an elegant interface; for many applications, we have not yet found a suitable replacement. In the meantime, digital technologies have provided us with access to more kinds of information, knowledge, and entertainment and indispensable ways to be productive and creative. I could not have written this book without a computer and MS Word. I marvel at the way great writers of the 19th century churned out their giant hand-written tomes. Apparently, Mark Twain was the first author to submit a typewritten manuscript to his publisher, Life on the Mississippi, in 1883; but for me the typewriter was a technology of no real short- or long-term value. I did not finish my PhD thesis because after two years of coursework and a master's thesis, I could not face typing another word. (But I'm also not too happy that I spent a ludicrous amount of time fixing widows on galley proofs.)

By our behavior—and by tracking and complying with market preferences—we have determined that the technologies that we have abandoned have no future value. Either by luck or unconscious competence but mostly due to market forces, we have ceased to maintain formats that we no longer need and are unlikely to make a comeback, like print newspapers, VHS, and eight-track cassettes. But we have also rescued some nearly obsolete technologies and welcomed their revival, like vinyl records. CDs too seem to retain some value to music collectors. Ham (amateur) radios and reel-to-reel tape recorders still appeal to hobbyists. We probably will not miss transistor radios, but we still want radios or at least a device that brings us radio broadcasts. Pagers are on the trash heap of obsolesced technologies, as are GPS devices, both replaced by smartphones.

We do not want to throw out the baby with the bath water, but we do need to change the water from time to time. So far, we have done a decent job of obsolescing the truly transitional formats that had little about them worth saving. Improved technologies and devices that have succeeded in the marketplace have given us more efficient access to information and knowledge than the technologies they have replaced.

If you were blind in the 18th century, you acquired most of your knowledge orally; at the time, there were no effective literacy tools for blind individuals. In 1785, the Frenchman Valentin Haüy expanded and improved on a tactile system for "reading" with embossed and movable characters that the Italian Jesuit Francesco Lana de Terzi had invented a century earlier. In 1819, another Frenchman, Charles Barbier de la Serre, created a system of raised dots on a grid and presented it at the Royal Institution of Blind Children. Though none of these earlier attempts at literacy solutions caught on, Louis Braille, who had blinded himself at the age of three, was a student at the Royal Institution at that time and set out to improve upon Barbier's system. In 1824, at the age of 15, Braille created the eponymous literacy code that is still used today.

Braille code consists of a series of six dots embossed, using interpoint printers, on heavyweight paper (sometimes embossed on both sides) and can be understood by users passing their fingers over the dots. For over a century blind and visually impaired people have gained access to books and written documents that have been converted into braille. Braille has enabled blind individuals to become literate and independent learners. And with the availability of audio technology, they have also had access to a much greater quantity and variety of information, knowledge, and entertainment from recorded books.

Visually challenged people relied exclusively on braille and conventional audio to gain access to the written word until the development of digital accessible information system (DAISY) technology in 1981. DAISY is a digital standard for audiobooks, periodicals, and computerized text, and provides a variety of features and functionality not available from an ordinary audio format. Commonly referred to as a Digital Talking Book (DTB) and designed specifically for people who are blind or have print disabilities, DTB files serve as a complete audio substitute for print material.

Since its inception, DTBs have continued to evolve with new features and functionality programmed in the files. They offer more than just standard audio renditions of text. Depending on the playback device, DTBs allow users to search, add bookmarks, navigate chapter by chapter or line by line, and regulate speaking speed. Users who are severely disabled but not totally blind can view images, as well as the text files, with additional screen-enlarging software and computer displays. Braille readers can access documents through a braille display device that can be connected to players specifically designed to read and play DTB files. DAISY technology also enables aurally accessible tables and graphics, which allow visually impaired listeners to navigate complex page layouts in textbooks and magazines not possible with conventional audio recordings. Digital Talking Books are designed specifically to expand the ability of blind and visually impaired users to access more information and read a variety of content sources.

The National Library of the Blind and Disabled, which is part of the Library of Congress, loans DTB players to patrons for free when they borrow recorded material from the Library of Congress collection. Based on their popularity and widespread usage, DTBs have provided a real boon to the blind community, especially given some of the constraints in the production and availability of braille-based content.

The process of converting books to braille relies on specialized interpoint printers, which are expensive, slow, and noisy. Braille books are much larger than ordinary books printed with ink on paper and require more pages for the equivalent information. (Apparently the *Bible* in braille takes up more than 100 volumes.) Because of the cost of producing books on braille and the limited size of the market, the number of available books in braille is a fraction of the number of regularly printed books. The Braille Institute's Library Services, a non-profit network coordinated by the Library of Congress, claims that they have 100,000 titles and 1.2 million volumes in the Library's collection, which is not a lot. Apparently only 1% of the world's literature has been printed in braille.[8] The lack of a sufficient number of books in braille has forced blind people who may have preferred to read in braille to turn to technology to access content that they need the most.

Braille advocates concede that developments in technology have made it cheaper and faster to read via a computer using screen-readers or use DTB players rather than braille. But what braille provides that technology-driven solutions for accessing information do not is the independence and control over the learning process—arguably what we all need for building confidence and to apply our knowledge. Perhaps in the same way as using computers has not replaced the need to learn to write by hand, DTBs do not replace the need for braille. I say "perhaps," because not being blind myself, I cannot possibly say for sure.

Braille champions argue that production technology (or the equivalent of digital printing for physical books) has improved the process of creating braille outputs, making it easier than ever to produce more braille books faster and cheaper. Today, using technology, visually challenged individuals can:

- Read any document on the Web with braille transcription software; text can be automatically transcribed into braille and printed in braille with a small interpoint printer.
- Access scanned braille documents connected to the National Library Service (NLS) and other digital libraries.
- Use a refreshable braille display (or braille terminal) with an embedded digital braille keyboard; the dots can raise or lower depending on the characters and the onscreen text can be directly translated onto the braille display.
- Use screen-reader software that converts the onscreen text into a braille page (or into a read-aloud text).

Further, the most enterprising technology users can produce braille books on their own. With the right combination of hardware and software, you can buy or borrow a book, scan it page by page creating a digital file, then use a screen-reader to render it into braille (or text-to-speech audio). The files can be downloaded onto a flash drive and inserted into a portable braille reader. In this way, hundreds of books can be stored and printed out in braille "on demand." But this is not for the typical braille user—at least not yet. But to a large degree, it does address digital literacy.

Technology has put the production of braille in the hands of the amateur printer, making braille easier to convert—with a compact embosser—and more portable by storing braille books and print materials on flash drives. These are all welcomed advances for readers of braille, giving them control over their learning and access to knowledge that they would not otherwise be able to have. But it still does not address the legacy content that should be made available to those who are visually impaired, as well as providing them with the ability to create more content more efficiently.

The emergence of portable wireless devices that scan text and translate it to braille means greater access to books and written information and more choices. But there is a larger problem facing braille other than finding more efficient ways to generate it. Although braille-producing technology is a benefit to braille readers, very few blind people can read braille, and because of a shortage of teachers, a declining number of people are learning it. According to the National Federation of the Blind, fewer than 10% of the 1.3 million people who are legally blind in the United States read braille. Only 10% of blind children are learning it. Further, each year as many as 75,000 people lose all or part of their vision, which means that as more baby-boom generation move into retirement age and as diabetes raises the risk of blindness, the NFB expects this number to increase dramatically. The concern is that without braille, illiteracy will also increase.[9]

Braille advocates worry about having to give up control over their learning in favor of the speed of absorbing text, which would mean sacrificing 100-plus years of literacy for the sake of gaining greater access to knowledge and information. Even though they recognize the benefits of DAISY and the difficulty in maintaining a community of braille users—including finding enough teachers and funding—much like the relationship that those of us who are not visually challenged have with print, many braille fans have a similar relationship with braille. For them, DAISY has not obsolesced braille. Here are some of the benefits of braille that advocates do not want to lose:

- Recorded speech is for speed, but braille is for accuracy.
- Braille can communicate layout information more efficiently than audio.
- It is easier to spot errors, like spelling mistakes, when reading braille, than it is to hear mispronunciations in speech.
- Braille provides intimacy with language. It might not be practical to read a ten-volume series in braille but reading a poem in braille is more desirable than audio, as is creating a label or quickly jotting something down.
- Braille, like print, does not need hardware or software, uses available light, does not need power to be read, and never crashes.

Readers of printed books, a much larger cohort of learners, did not have to make these sacrifices when adopting other technologies for gaining access to knowledge. For print readers, the technology solutions have been additive. Braille users are not Luddites; on the contrary, they have embraced technology and the access to information and knowledge that it has enabled. But many braille advocates do not want to lose a tool that has not only survived for more than 100 years but continues to offer a unique value. They want to keep what they have and take advantage of the best technology available. Still, maintaining an ongoing production of braille books may be a problem given the high costs and low demand.

Fifteen years ago, when I was still developing curriculum products, I had submitted a middle school math program for a state adoption. To be ADA (Americans with Disabilities Act) compliant, the RFP required that we produce a version that would be accessible to the visually challenged students. As expensive as it is to create a braille version of a textbook, it is exponentially harder and more expensive to do it with a four-color math book. The adoption committee gave us the choice to produce either a braille version or a DTB. We chose the latter, and had the series converted into DAISY, which was a relatively painless process.

With the declining number of braille users, and the difficulty in finding qualified teachers, braille may not play a significant role in developing literacy skills for visually challenged people in the future. Still, I would not give up on paper, which has proven to be a versatile and long-lasting medium. It accepts text, images, and color; it can be folded creatively (and used to create pop-up books), stamped, and embossed. If it is heavy enough, it can be embossed on both sides. With primitive interpoint printers—and without computers and software—Louis Braille created a tactile landscape of literacy, literally raising words off the page.

We generally think of digital solutions as pixels on a screen or as sound files, with additional hardware devices to gain access to digital content. But paper can be a digital medium as well. "Smart paper" can retain digital information and provide a direct link between the physical and digital worlds. Smart paper, which looks and feels just like normal paper (and is no heavier), uses radio frequency tags that are embedded into the paper and that can be read by devices with sensors, like decoder "pens" or smartphones to link to the Internet, display images, or produce sound. The tags are nearly invisible and do not change the look or feel of the paper. Using special conductive ink, regular paper can be converted into smart paper during the printing process to produce an interactive book that can talk or link to websites to create virtual reality experiences.

Five years ago, I worked with a publisher to develop a six-book science series for kids that used smart paper. Every page in each of the books contained a hidden world of multimedia that was released when touched by a decoder pen that would make the page come alive with music and speech. Using specially designed goggles and a smart phone, virtual reality images can be produced with the same technology.

There was a time when our only option for acquiring information and knowledge was with print, and we defined literacy as the ability to read and write. These are critical socializing skills that help to pave our road to personal growth and success in the world. But in the future, the acquisition of knowledge may not depend on alpha-numeric literacy. Before the written word we had an oral tradition. Perhaps the digital era will create new avenues of access with accelerated levels of digital literacy.

I return to Richard Wurman's view, which I cited in Chapter 2, on the methods we use to acquire knowledge and evolve as an inclusive society, and what he identifies as the age of also: "There's not a best way of communicating. There's not a best way for anything. There are just good ways."

Notes

1. This quote is from *The Lives of William Benton*, by Sidney Hyman. The University of Chicago Press, 1969. Although Hyman's book refers to the years up to the publication of his book, Britannica's educational film division continued to grow throughout the 1970s and dominated the educational film market through most of the 1980s until movies in VHS took over. Britannica produced their last film in 1995.
2. The *Wikipedia* article on the Britannica films recognizes the collection's unique value:
   The higher-than-average quality of EB films have enjoyed renewed interest as some titles gradually fell into public domain and are easily viewed on YouTube and the Internet Archive. Because the company made comparatively fewer social guidance films than [its] rivals . . . (the type that are often ridiculed today with the changing social customs) and the producers were [extremely] cautious in their choices of narration and music, many of these films tend to be viewed as less "dated" today than other non-theatrical ephemerals.
3. AFANA is the only institution in the United States dedicated solely to documenting the history of the 16-mm classroom academic film.
4. Quotes are from the Benton Institute for Broadband & Society website, March 14, 2021, https://www.benton.org/about-benton.
5. OC Inc. website: http://www.uccmediajustice.org/, March 14, 2021.
6. The first Librarian of Congress was appointed in 1802 by then President Thomas Jefferson. Billington's tenure as the 13th Librarian of Congress lasted 28 years, from 1987 to 2015.
7. Taken from the Library of Congress, NAVCC website, March 15, 2021, https://www.loc.gov/programs/audio-visual-conservation/.
8. Peter White, "Digital Books May Not Be for Everyone. But for Blind People, They're a True Revolution," *The Guardian*, August 17, 2012.
9. From *Facing the Truth, Reversing the Trend, Empowering the Blind*, Report to the Nation by the National Federation of the Blind Jernigan Institute, March 26, 2009.

INDEX

Academic Film Archive of North America 165–6
adoption cycle 70–2, 89
advertising 3, 7, 158
"age of also" 43–4, 46
Alexander, Geoff 165–6
alphabetical listings 2–5, 12, 19
alpha-numerical naming convention 3–5
Amazon 33, 36, 46, 56, 121; ASIN 56–7; Kindle 41, 46; Kindle Direct Publishing 131–4; Prime 61
Americans with Disabilities Act 175
Andersen, Lene Rachel 95
Apple 9, 121, 154
apps 40–1, 45, 49, 95–6
artificial intelligence 27–8, 45, 58–9
Association of American Publishers 65
Association of Educational Publishers 65
atlases 9
audiobooks 45–6, 49–50, 57, 121–3, 139, 142–3, 151

automation 27–8

bandwidth 127
Barnes and Noble 10
BBC 76
Beekman, Tim 127
Benton, Charles 162–70
best-selling authors 130
Beta tapes 125–6
Big Data 53
Billington, James 167
Birrell, Augustine 137
BISAC subject codes 56–8
blended learning 139
blogs 50, 53
book-of-the-month clubs 10–11
books see e-books; print books
bookstores 10, 23
Booktopia 56
braille 100, 122, 171–6
Braille, Louis 171, 176
Braille Institute 173
Brand, Stewart 154

INDEX

Britannica 12–13, 15, 18–23, 86–7, 98, 100, 144, 151–2, 162–6, 168–9; Digital Learning 87
Bruzzone, Catherine 33–4, 47–8
business models 18, 23, 31, 77, 96, 104, 135

card catalogues 164
Carnegie, Andrew 137
cartography *see* maps
catalogues 29
CD-ROMs 6–7, 18–23, 31, 42–6, 57, 105
Cohen, Betsy 109–16
compact discs 29, 31, 44, 49, 123–4, 139, 150, 171
Conan Doyle, Arthur 53
Consortium for School Networking 65
copyright 17, 98, 100, 116, 167–8
Covid-19 pandemic 35, 76–80, 82–3, 101–2, 104, 109–15, 128–9, 139, 146–7
Cracchiolo, Rachelle 82–4
Creative Commons 116–18
Creative Structures 41, 45
crowd-sourcing 22
Crump, Simon 27–8
customer expectations 93–7
customer lifetime value 88, 93, 95
customer satisfaction 86–102

DAISY 122, 172, 174–5
Dale, Jim 122–4
data 53–62
data entry 27, 105–6
de la Serre, Charles Barbier 171
de Terzi, Francesco Lana 171
Dee, Thomas 66–7
dictionaries 6–7, 11, 29, 43–4

"digital first" principle 54–5
digital natives 65
digital printers 32–7
Digital Promise 65
digital rights management 140
digital talking books 172–3, 175
Disney Plus 11
Ditlow, Tim 122–5
Doerr, John 51
DOMO 53
DVD-ROMs 6, 18, 22
DVDs 38, 44, 126, 139, 150–1, 163

EAN 56
e-books 30, 37–8, 74–6, 86–7, 93–4, 131–2; libraries and 40–1, 47, 138–52; print-digital hybrids 40–51
EdTech 64–84, 88–9, 95–6, 104, 129, 151
Education Research & Development Institute 65
edWeb 77–8
edX 119
Einstein, Albert 86, 103
Emerson, Ralph Waldo 121
Encarta 20–2
Encyclopaedia Britannica Educational Company 162
encyclopedias 10–23, 29, 87, 144
epub 46
e-serials 139
e-zines 94, 115, 121

Facebook 7
flipped classrooms 139
Floyd, George 114
freemium models 159–60
Funk & Wagnall's New Encyclopedia 20, 22

Gates, Bill and Melinda 137
Golden, Ken 123–5
Google 9, 61–2; Classroom 75, 80; Forms 80; Meet 76, 104, 116; Play 121; Translate 99
GPS systems 9, 55–6, 171
GrandPré, Mary 124
Grant, Ian 41–2, 45
Green Comma 117–18
Gulf Oil Company 8

hardback books 45–6
Hardy, Jerome 10–11
Harry Potter 122–5, 130
Haüy, Valentin 171
HBO 11, 61, 156
Hillwig, Phyllis 129–30
Hive 56
Hoopla 148, 151
Howey, Hugh 131
Hulu 61
hyperlinks 43

ImageQuest 98–100
Ingram 56
Institute for the Study of Knowledge Management in Education 117
intellectual property 47, 61, 101, 143
international markets 97–102
International Society for Technology in Education 65
Intrator, Peggy 100–1
iPads 40–1, 148
ISBN 56–7, 131

just in time 27

Kanopy 148
Kindle 41, 46
Kindle Direct Publishing 131–4

Klinenberg, Eric 137
Koller, Daphne 119

learning management content systems 74
learning management systems 66, 74–5, 80, 88, 99, 145
Learning Object Repository 128
Lee, Jennifer 123–5
legacy print products 19, 22, 54–5, 57, 86, 134, 174
lexicon 95
libraries 9–10, 13, 16, 23, 36, 38, 47, 56, 58, 61–2, 87–8, 98, 119, 137–52, 155, 166; apps and e-books 40–1, 47, 138–52
Library of Congress 149, 167–9, 172–3
Library Video Company 126–7
LibraryPass 146–7
Listening Library 122–4
literacy 175–6

magazines 9, 29, 50, 108–9, 155; digital (*see* e-zines)
MapQuest 9
maps 8–9, 20, 22–3; digital 9, 139
market adaptability 37
marketing 3, 61, 87, 116, 132
Marx, Anthony 149
Massive Open Online Courses 119–20
MEDLINE database 62
Mehta, Dushyant 36
Merriam-Webster 43
metadata 27, 55–61, 105, 132
microform 139
micropublishers 53
Microsoft 20–2
Midwest Tape 151
monetization 58, 61, 116, 169
Morganthaler, Lynelle 78–80

Morse, John 43–4
MP3 downloads 29, 31
multimedia 121–36, 176
multinational publishers 97–8

National Assessment of Educational Progress 68
National Audio-Visual Conservation Center 167–9
National Center for Education Statistics 68
National Federation of the Blind 174
National Library of the Blind and Disabled 172
National Library Service 173
Netflix 11, 61, 156
newsletters 114–15
newspapers 10, 23, 30, 44, 54, 108, 155, 171; digital 94, 121, 156
Ng, Andrew 119
Norvig, Peter 119

offset printing 32–4
one-to-many distribution model 23, 30, 37–8
one-to-one distribution model 23, 30, 37–8
ONIX database 56
online distributors 36; *see also individual companies*
Open Educational Resources Commons 117–19
Open-Source Software 118
Oxford English Dictionary 6, 11

paper costs 30, 32
paper mills 2, 7, 32
paperback books 45–6, 57
paywalls 55, 61–2, 166
PBS 76
PCs 21–2

Pickering, Ruth 58–9
piracy 47
podcasts 31, 50, 116, 121–2
pre-press 27, 36
pricing models 154–60
print books 27–39, 170–1; hardbacks 45–6; legacy print products 19, 22, 54–5, 57, 86, 134, 174; paperbacks 45–6, 57; print-digital hybrids 40–51, 73; (*see also* CD-ROMs); supply chain 7, 18, 27–8, 32, 36–8, 133; textbooks 66, 71–4; encyclopedias 13, 18, 20; *see also* dictionaries
print-digital hybrids 40–51, 73; *see also* CD-ROMs
printing presses 7, 32
print-on-demand 27, 33–7, 130
problem identification 103–20
public domain 75, 130–1, 166
PubMed 62

radio 9, 31, 171
Rand McNally 8–9
remote learning *see* virtual learning
Repro India 36–7
return on investment 37, 39, 97, 143, 152, 170
Rivero, Victor 35
road maps *see* maps
Ross, Marshall 133–6
Rowling, J. K. 122–4, 130
royalties 36–7, 47

SAFARI Montage 127–8
Schlessinger, Andrew 126–8
Schlessinger Media 126–7
Schmucki, Lisa 77–8
search capabilities 7, 18, 43, 144
search engine marketing 61

INDEX

search engine optimization 61
search engines 5, 7, 22, 56, 61; *see also* metadata
Sears, Roebuck 12
self-publishing 33, 46, 53, 121, 130–6
Shah, Amit 117–18
Shark Tank 103–4
sheet-fed offset printers 32
short-run printing 33–4
Singer, Ian 146–7
single sign-on 74, 145, 166
smart paper 176
smartphones 66, 171, 176
Smith, Bill 107–19
Smith Bigham, Vicki 80–1, 89–93, 104–6, 108
social and emotional learning 109–10, 113
social media 7, 116, 142
software as a service 96, 166
"space patrol" 16
Springer Nature 97–8
State Educational Technology Directors Association 65
Stein, Gertrude 64
streaming services 11, 29, 31, 61, 121, 143, 156
subscriptions, online 11
supply chain 7, 18, 27–8, 32, 36–8, 133

Teacher Created Materials 82–3
telephone directories 2–8, 23, 29
telephone operators 6
telephony 2–8
television 9, 31, 44
textbooks 66, 71–4
Thrun, Sebastien 119
time to market 37

Time-Life Books 10–12
total cost of ownership 34
trade shows 84
training 80–4, 96
travel guidebooks 9
Tri-Plex Packaging 123–5
Twain, Mark 171
Two-Can 44–5

Underground Vaults & Storage 161–6, 169–70
United Learning and Aims 127
UPC 56
UPS 15
user generated content 117

Valery, Paul 27
value chain 28
VHS 38, 125–6, 163, 166, 171
video 125–8, 139
vinyl records 29, 31
virtual learning 76–80, 104, 128–9
virtual reality 45
virtual training 81–4
vlogs 53

Walmart 36
Walsh, Kate 122
Walters, Jennie 132–3
web offset printers 32
websites 49–51, 61–2, 73, 86–7, 95, 105–6, 108, 121, 149–50
Westlaw 11
Wightwick, Jane 49–50
Wikipedia 22–3, 117
Wilde, Oscar 154
Windows 21–2
workshops 114
World Almanac 29

World Book Encyclopedia 12–13, 15, 18–22, 44
Wozniak, Steve 154–5
Wurman, Richard Saul 43–4, 46, 176

Xfinity 61

yearbooks 16–17
yellow pages 2–5
Yewno 58–60
Youth Communication 108–16

Zoom 76, 80, 104, 114, 116, 129, 149